D0946748

A SWINGER OF BIRCHES

A Swinger of Birches

A PORTRAIT OF ROBERT FROST

By Sidney _Cox_

With an introduction by Robert Frost

NEW YORK UNIVERSITY PRESS

Washington Square · New York

Quotations from Complete Poems of Robert Frost
(*Copyright 1930, 1939 by Holt, Rinehart and Win-
ston, Inc.*) *are reprinted by permission of Holt,
Rinehart and Winston, Inc.*

For Alice
the other I've tried hardest to understand

Introduction

This ought to be a good book. Everybody who has seen it in manuscript says it is. The author probably knew me better than he knew himself and consequently contrariwise he very likely portrayed himself in it more than me. I trust it is in my favor. I know he would mean it to be. I don't read about myself well or easily. But I am always happier to hear that I am liked faults and all than that I am disliked. I had to tell Sidney once that I didn't believe it did me the least good to be told of the enemies he had had to defend me from. I have stolen look enough over the edge of the book to see that what went on between us is brought out much as in our correspondence. My letters to him I might mention are on deposit in the Dartmouth College Library. I wish I had kept some of the great letters he wrote me but I am no curator of letters or anything else. He was at his best in his free letters. Yes, and of course in his teaching. A great teacher. He was all sincerity and frankness. He once wrote an article for the *New Republic* about *my* sincerity. I know that because it was in the title. We differed more in taste perhaps than in thinking. But we stood up to each other to support each other as two playing cards may be made to in building. I am a great equalitarian: I try to spend most of my time with my equals. He seemed worried at first lest it should appear I didn't seek him as much as he sought me. He respected me very highly. And he was more serious about such things than I. Not that he lacked a sense of humor. He liked a good story, and I am sure he would have enjoyed my version of our first encounter. It began one evening in 1911 when we met as strangers looking on at a school dance at Plymouth, New Hampshire, where we were both teachers, he in one school, I in another. I didn't know who he was except that he looked very teasably young. He didn't know who I was except, it seems, that I looked too old. By saying something flippant about the theme papers he had to hurry away to correct I angered him to the point of his inquiring behind my back if it was because of alcohol I had got no further up in the world at my age. I was thirty-seven. I was just teaching psychology in the Plymouth Normal School. He disdained to speak to me on the street for a while afterwards. But his seriousness piqued the mischief in me and I set myself to take him. He came round all right, but it wasn't the last time he had to make allowances for me. He worked at it devotedly. He must have been about half my age then. He was all of two thirds my age when he died. He was catching up. He was cut off before he came all the way through with himself. But he had made up his mind to much. My heart was in his literary success and I have hopes this is it.

Robert Frost

Contents

Preface

This book attempts a portrait of the wholeness of a man. It concentrates the effort of almost forty years. It is conditioned by the fact that all that time he has seemed to me the most lively and understanding and coherently constructive man I have known. Much of the time I have had long, hard struggles composing my conclusions with his. And I end very different from him. But, for better or for worse, I still think him the wisest man, and one of the two deepest and most honest thinkers, I know. I may be handicapped by my affection; I am also aided by it in the urge to master and understand.

He and I long ago agreed that if I wrote a book about him it should leave out biography and strive to get the ideas. Another friend might do a full consideration of his poetry. There is nothing here that he suggested putting in. He and I are, strange as it may appear, on the best of terms—without his being made unnatural by the existence of this attempt and without my putting understanding above affection. I have never produced a notebook on him.

When I use quotes and say Robert Frost said, I am giving his exact words. When I say Robert Frost said without using quotes, I am giving you vivid memories of what he said, with many of his exact words, but, insecure about accuracy, I refuse to use quotes. In a few instances the directly quoted passages are based on somebody else's quotation marks.

"I'd rather know four or five poems than all of anybody's understanding of those poems."

ROBERT FROST

". . . who nailed words to their primitive senses, as farmers drive down stakes in the spring, which the frost has heaved; who derived his words as often as he used them,—transplanted them to his page . . . ; whose words were so true and fresh and natural that they would appear to expand like the buds at the approach of spring, though they lay half-smothered between two musty leaves in a library, —aye to bloom there, after their kind annually, for the faithful reader, in sympathy with surrounding Nature."

HENRY DAVID THOREAU

A SWINGER OF BIRCHES

I

Robert Frost has never been the fashion

Robert Frost never let his head get caught in a halo. He never stood still for admirers to pull a laurel wreath down over his eyes. He kept free to exchange a taunt and a you-and-I-both wink with rogues and the repressed rascal in nearly all of us. He has let nothing come between him and the funny world.

That slight offishness of his in part accounts for the success of his poems in the Armed Services edition, in Pocket Books, and in the Modern Library. It partly accounts, too, for the fact that no philosopher or artist is better worth listening to, no writer so well worth reading. But his slight offishness, his refusal "to adapt" himself "a mite," also accounts for his being out of fashion.

But he has never been in fashion. In spite of all the honorary degrees, memberships in academies and international societies, individual awards and Pulitzer prizes, in spite of his large place in most anthologies, Robert Frost has never been in fashion. The solemnly serious have either bracketed him with Whittier, or vainly tried, as Amy Lowell did, to fit him to a program, or dismissed him for failing to writhe in verse.

For twenty years he went undiscovered while George Herbert Palmer waved away "The Death of the Hired Man" and Richard Hovey told him how to make his poems poetic. His poems, Hovey told him, had too much the sounds of speech. In 1914 Stuart Sherman couldn't see much in *A Boy's Will*, though later his eyes cleared. And after *North of Boston* some reader remarked, in each successive volume, a falling off. From the first it was plain that such "preternatural self-confidence" would not become the fashion.

In 1951 Robert Frost's thinking was no more incorrigible than it was in 1911, when I first felt, on frequent walks or talking late at night, the gentle challenge of his common sense against my idealism, the terrible surprise of his subtle discrimination against my simplifying. He continues about the same distance from the approved line of thought that independent minds should follow with one accord.

Mirth has always been attendant on his moral. He will not, for earnest half-truths, stay completely reverent. He has to keep the door ajar for the other half of the truth. Even in his caperings that irk the solemn and embarrass the earnest, wisdom is usually implicit. Trifling is pertinent, though often it seems pesky, when dealing with inflated trifles. And even with God, the fear of not pleasing whom is the beginning of wisdom,

Robert Frost sets his soft hat on one side of his head and looks Him in the eye.

As always, he is saying to his readers, The like of this, according to your natures, you, too, could do and preserve your poise. He said in conversation before he ever said in verse: "The one indecency's to make a fuss." For the overhopeful there seems a sinister cynicism in his sly reiteration that life is really always like the life we find so terrifying. They defensively resent his quiet assumption that finding a way to take life with similar conflicts and identical elements is just the perennial human enterprise.

The two books of 1947 are neither obscure nor lacking in the highest seriousness for those who took "time out for reassembly" when they read his earlier *Masque of Reason.* But you had to read with susceptibility to being altered slightly in your fundamentals. In the earlier masque you had to go through the change of first agreeing with Job that

> *We don't know where we are, or who we are.*
> *We don't know one another; don't know You;*
> *Don't know what time it is.*

Then, slowly but finally, you have to whirl with Job and Robert Frost, confidently questioning the absoluteness of despair.

> *We don't know, don't we?*
>
> . . . .
>
> *Oh, we know well enough to go ahead with.*

A reader who reaches down to the deep truth of knowing "enough to go ahead with" is ready at last to assent that

> there's no such thing as Earth's becoming
> An easier place for man to save his soul in.
> Except as a hard place to save his soul in,
> A trial ground where he can try himself
> And find out whether he is any good,
> It would be meaningless.

Natural intelligence, unbiased by any system, is necessary in reading original authors. We have to continue alive enough to budge a little from our own point of view. Every time Robert has read me a new poem it has brought almost to my lips the pedant or the prude. But isn't it a shade crude? I have at first thought. Or too colloquial? Or a trace facetious? Or rather inconclusive? Or slightly harsh? Or a little too modest? But if my objection had been removed, the fidelity of the poem to all the unstated incompatibles would have been diminished. As Robert wrote it, the poem could never seem too simple or too cosmic to be true. We have to grow in order to like great poems. We have to start imagining a new way.

Robert Frost offers us nothing cozier to join than America. He firmly pushes off all attempts to snuggle into his point of view. He obstinately declines to be a supplier of formulas. It would be absurd for him to think of pronouncing finally.

"The evidence is almost in," he says. And all he will declare, as, according to him, poets have always declared, is "Sometimes it seems as if . . ."

II

He's too original

Robert Frost always cared about the news, though. He is the more alert now because he remembers much and is not tethered to the little hour. What he represents is the most various sensitiveness and the common sense of the times. It is not the slightly musty forms of thought and taste newly arrived in the little magazines and at the universities.

In the summer of 1915 when he was just back from England and known to those most on the lookout for some new thing in literature, a singularly able young PH.D. made a pilgrimage to Franconia to investigate. The budding professor had little firsthand acquaintance with life. He seemed to feel that he had missed, muffed, and muddled much that he had been exposed to. He had been too busy learning from libraries.

The poet had gleaned more from fewer books; he had been finding things out by encounters along his own way. He had always known that "Life must be kept up at a great rate in order to absorb any considerable amount of learning."

Being included in this young scholar's tour among the celebrities in poetry was life, Robert felt, new and exciting, a challenge. Could he be shown? Most likely not. At least he could be welcomed into Robert's life a day or two. He put the stiff young Doctor of Philosophy at ease. There was no effusiveness, Robert was not too naïvely glad that he was there on account of the poems. He accepted him with casual hospitality and fully met him, not as a type but as a person.

At first the professor did most of the talking. He spoke intelligently of the poems in *North of Boston*. He realized that the man with tousled hair, open-collared homemade shirt, creaseless pants, and comfortable old shoes was worthy of his steel, and he did not hold back his stock of positive ideas, his store of precise facts.

Robert Frost talked facts, too. His judgments were implicit in a story or backed up by cases. But what a quiet observer noticed, underlying, was the gentle, playful sureness of the reality of the undefined. It was that sureness, most of all, that he had in common with the poem he called the greatest poem in English in recent years. "The Listeners" by Walter de la Mare affirmed the reality of the undefined.

But what the professor was interested in was the defined. He was full of disapproval of social conditions, and he had much to say of remedies. About the remedies Robert was skeptical. He indicated evils worse than the conditions that the remedies might bring on. What hope there was lay in the power of man's desire: to accept, select, and rearrange. Conditions, after all, were the setting of the human play. We wouldn't want to reform away our chances to demonstrate that we are men. We couldn't if we did.

About progress Robert wondered. Except in matters of comfort and speed his guess was that we hadn't got far beyond Plato. We hadn't got far in thought and feeling. Or had we?

Oh yes, that was one thing the young professor thought there could be no doubt about. Enlightenment was slow, but it was spreading. We were getting rid of the old taboos, the fear of the supernatural was weakening, the primacy of reason was more generally acknowledged, art was more and more directed to the solution of the human problem, and when the profit motive had been discredited and war eliminated progress would be swifter. Look at George Meredith. Look at the new movement in poetry. Look at Ibsen.

Would he say, Robert wanted to know, that Ibsen represented an advance over Shakespeare?

Indeed he did. Shakespeare had the rich tapestry of feudalism to work with, the opulence of the Renaissance, the new amplitude and buoyancy of the spacious days of good Queen Bess. He was "sweetest Shakespeare, fancy's child." But Ibsen had ideas.

The difference between Shakespeare and Ibsen, Robert said, is that Shakespeare never but once wrote formula first. Shakespeare got interested in a situation, started playing with it, and had fun manipulating it, seeing people come alive, and drawing parallels to his observation and experience. At last the meaning that had caused him to be interested, the inherent idea, was developed in his mind—often to a formula. Modern dramatists like Ibsen at his worst and Shaw always (1915) start formula first. And so story and character are "warped, warped, warped." He showed it happening in *The Master Builder*. No; formula first had better be left to people with something to sell and sociological preachers. It was a way of cheating without feeling guilty.

The professor uncrossed his legs, found his cigarette case, and offered Robert a cigarette. While the professor took long drags Robert held his in his hand, slid a little farther down in his Morris chair, and went on to say that even poets who write what is praised for stark realism sometimes get their stuff by speculation, too. His friend in England, Wilfrid Gibson, was writing about working people and their wives—miners, for example. Gibson admitted that he had never known a miner, had never been near a coal mine. He wrote of what they must be like. All conjecture. Robert shook his head, smiling.

He reached over to a table and picked up two or three thin volumes with bright dust jackets. He read here and there, sympathetically, doing full justice. But the headshake came more often than the approving comment. Poeticisms and poetic flummeries he made rubbish of.

The talk turned to earlier American poets, and Robert characterized several of them. After a while the young professor asked him if he wasn't afraid that such awfully severe standards would arouse antagonism. Why, they would hardly leave us anyone but Poe, Whitman, and Emerson.

But he couldn't take a vigorous stand on patriotic grounds. Patriotism was—in his new theory—one of the things we were outgrowing, along with sentimentality in general.

Robert took occasion in one of their many talks to distinguish between sound sentiment and sentimentality. It was plain by now that he would not be tender with false sentiment. It was in quite another connection that Robert said it was all right with him if people held back against their emotions, like a farmer leaning back to check the horse at the far end of a furrow. But we couldn't dismiss emotions. We wouldn't want to. We needed horsepower for the plough. To have it, though, we had to wait for real feelings. Larruped emotions couldn't be trusted. In matters like patriotism and love we wished for a feeling that we'd heard about, and we wanted it so badly that we went ahead and had it by the straining of determination, instead of because we couldn't help it. That was silly. The feelings that give us power and lead to wisdom are the feelings we can't help having.

About that time Mrs. Frost couldn't help having a feeling. "Rob," she said, "it's after nine o'clock, and you *must* go milk. It's not good for her to wait so long." Her sweet voice was low and a little sad.

When Robert came back in, he lighted a round-wicked lamp, turning it up carefully, and proposed to read a little poetry. The professor welcomed the suggestion, pressed out his cigarette, and made his long thin body comfortable. Robert read in talking tones, following the curve and play of feeling, as people with some reserve speak when they have their hearts in what they say. In reading "The Hound of Heaven" his voice ran with the emotion, wound through labyrinths, darted, plunged, and yielded at last to the caressing hand and pursuing forgiveness. Every flick and flicker of emotion was made audible. Between poems Robert paused occasionally for an anecdote about the poet, if the poet happened to be one he had known in England. And he and the professor swapped comments.

Robert said that the words in poems must always be inevitable, never used because they are fine.

Every poem of his, he said, was based on an actual experience. The tent the visitor had noticed in the yard was the one mentioned in "A Servant to Servants." Some of the people in his poems had discovered themselves there, he said. Of course he altered combinations and put names and places together contrary to the map. In "The Mountain" the mountain's name comes from another place, and the town is not Lunenberg but one in Vermont near Lake Willoughby, where he stayed one summer to avoid ragweed and hay fever.

After another poem the visitor returned to poetic license, and Robert said: "A poet must lean hard on facts, so hard, sometimes, that they hurt." He declined, he said, the traditional license. But since he did, since he rejected the old and respectable tradition that poetry was superior to facts, above them, and at liberty to set them aside, he couldn't feel himself abused by the long indifference of publishers to his new sort of poetry.

He didn't want anyone, he said, to treat him as an exhibit against American taste. His going to England wasn't any shaking the dust of his own country off his feet. It was just a happening that he had been published in England first. The *Independent* had taken poems of his twenty years before his first book. And so had three or four other periodicals.

One poet, the visitor said, who had similar views about fidelity to the facts was J. M. Synge, the Irish poet and playwright.

Yes, Robert said, he liked to read his *Playboy of the Western World*. But there was a difference. You wouldn't catch him listening to talk through a chink in the floor of an upstairs room and setting the talk down in a notebook, the way Synge did on one of the Isles of Aran. The thing is to notice good things because they catch your ear and fancy. Among the rank and file of any country there are unknown makers of shrewd phrases and sayings that salt down experience. A poet should have an ear for them and catch the spirit of them. Without a notebook he would remember them at appropriate instants, and he would also become able to make some himself that readers could not tell from the uncultivated ones.

Mrs. Frost had excused herself and gone off to bed, and the professor had had a day of it. He had better be getting back to the Forest Hills House. He had insured himself against intruding—and also against the discomforts of unaccustomed rusticity—by taking a room there before he climbed the hill for his visit. A little embarrassedly he let Robert know that he dreaded the walk down the solitary tree-bordered road in the dark. His too well organized world of concepts and formulas had sprung a little; he wasn't sure that something unpredicted might not slink through. Unorganized nature he had small means of coping with. And so Robert and I went down with him, feeling out the dusty road and smelling the raspberries and fir balsams, until he was safely under Franconia's village lights.

For two days more he visited. He went swimming with us, and heard about the time in England that Robert almost drowned, and listened to the scientific explanation of a wave. On the way back up the hill he heard Robert sing "Blow the Man Down." He stayed to lunch and dinner. He napped in the tent. And there was much talk and reading. Most of the time he and Robert were alone together. He had many shocks.

He heard Robert soberly remarking on the prevalence of no belief, heard him praise his friend William Ernest Hocking's *Meaning of God in Human Experience*, heard Mrs. Frost say she believed in immortality, and heard Robert say so did he; he believed it with an "almost physical certainty." And when the visitor began to raise the usual doubts, he heard Robert declare that he had no proofs to offer; logical systems of thought were nonsense; even the most impersonal processes were determined largely by influences controlling the logician but altogether excluded from the system and ignored; the shaping of our thought depends mainly on the premise we start with and what we take next, since all things in the universe are related.

The professor had a foretaste of much of the ripened thinking in *A Masque of Reason.* He also heard Robert doubting the beneficence of widespread birth control and hoping that among the leavening traits that New England provides America, along with "the ideals that will make our country great," would be the welcoming of large families. To have geniuses and powerful men, Robert said, a people must have many children. A small proportion will be exceptional, and the chances of a genius could not be controlled by eugenics. If a bright man and woman had ten children and a dull man and woman the same number, the dull family was as likely to contain the genius.

No wonder the professor said Robert was an anarchist. He had never heard a literate man make light of so many of the bright new ideas and intellectual fashions of the day. Almost everything he had assumed in his glib early talking on that visit had been questioned or countered before it was time to say good-by. And yet he had not been contradicted; there had been no arguments. And there had never been a quarter of an hour that he hadn't known that the man he talked with and listened to was more variously aware, more insusceptible of self-deception, and more successful in preserving sensitiveness than any of the scholars, literary men, and brilliant minds that he had known.

But Robert Frost was human. He had prejudices. He liked to be right, and he paid small heed to the convention that one speaks only well of rivals. In fact, as the visitor then saw it, Robert Frost violated several of the requirements of the well-bred man. But surely he was a man. And surely he was gentle. No one had ever made each thing said seem so specially for him —for the particular person he addressed. No one had ever guessed his feelings so rightly and answered not his words but the feelings. No one with anything like the same force and momentum had ever so avoided crowding or stunning him. He had taken him seriously. Even the way he laughed, sometimes, at the things the visitor had said was really showing faith in him. He didn't have a modern mind. He might be a little crude—or raw—or new. Yes, new. The able future critic was perplexed, but a new friendship had commenced. Robert saw through him all right. And he didn't see anything that wasn't there; he was too genuine and clear-seeing to be fooled. But his seeing what was there made it swell like a sun-stirred seed.

In some such whirl of reflections as this, it may be, the future able critic requested signed copies of the first two books of poems and asked for a photograph. And as he parted from his host at the bottom of the hill, and looked back at him, large, resolute, and balanced, he may have thought: "I guess he is right. Original would be a better word."

III

"Originality . . . was of the Devil"

Robert Frost has gone against a lot of good advice. He disappointed expectations. After he was married, his grandfather still considered him a good-for-naught. Robert had some grounds in his experience for his ambiguous winking eye, some claim to free-masonry with the not quite legal.

He accepted the unceasing struggle within himself as well as between himself and circumstances and conditions, and smiled in advance at the ridiculous minuteness and ambiguity of accomplishment, and got ready to write "Pertinax":

> *Let chaos storm!*
> *Let cloud shapes swarm!*
> *I wait for form.*

He thought of poetry—and behaved, sometimes, as if he thought of life—as a prank. He wanted poetry to play pranks on prevailing fictions. In 1945 he used the word "prank" also in the other, older sense; he wanted poetry to prank or deck the world. And to be free for pranks he had to assume full responsibility.

But in this world, he felt, there must always be leeway for the unregenerate. There must be elbow-room, even though someone may use it, cruelly, to swing a cat. In the Preface he wrote for the republished *Memoirs of the Notorious Stephen Burroughs*, in 1924, he enjoyed bracketing himself with that canting impostor.

"We bad people I should say had appearances to keep up no less dangerously than the good." And he proceeded to expose the falsity of attempts of men like Burroughs "to pass for large-hearted." But Robert Frost is always serious in his joking. He has a very serious intent in suggesting that Burroughs' book be put on "the same shelf with Franklin and Jonathan Edwards (grandfather of Aaron Burr). Franklin will be a reminder of what we have been as a young nation in some respects, Edwards in others. Burroughs comes in reassuringly when there is question of our not unprincipled wickedness, whether we have enough of it for salt. The world knows we are criminal enough. We commit our share of blind and inarticulate murder, for instance. But sophisticated wickedness, the kind that knows its grounds and can twinkle—could we be expected to have produced so fine a flower in a pioneer state? The answer is that we had it and had it early in Stephen Burroughs (not to mention Aaron Burr). It is not just a recent publisher's importation from Europe."

IV

He jarred our similes

Robert Frost's originality strikes us as devilish also because he fails to use a simile that we use constantly and have come to regard not as figurative but factual. Progress is our chief "native simile"; we always knew that life was like a stream, a road, a voyage, a flight, a racecourse.

But Robert Frost wrote in 1925: "The most exciting movement in nature is not progress, advance, but the expansion and contraction, the opening and shutting of the eye, the hand, the heart, the mind. We throw our arms wide with a gesture of religion to the universe; we close them around a person. We explore and adventure for a while and then draw in to consolidate our gains. The breathless swing is between subject matter and form."

Not getting somewhere. Not reaching our goal. Not getting ahead. Not paving the way for our children.

Not furthering social ends. Not setting more distant goals. Not marching all together to our glorious destiny.

Opening and shutting, throwing our arms wide and closing them, exploring and adventuring, then drawing in to consolidate.

You couldn't call it nonconformity. It is dual conformity. In expanding you conform to the raw nature of things. You come against the nettles and the down; you are terrified by the whirlwind and lulled by the rocking wave. Then you contract and consolidate. You take all that outside experience and gradually shape it. You shape it with your whole past and all your desires and determinations.

V

He swings birches

Robert Frost still won't be taken for a serious thinker. He says today he'd like his masques to be thought of as similar to Oscar Wilde's *Importance of Being Ernest* and Max Beerbohm's short story "E. V. Laider." It is not important like doctrine; it is only play with great ideas. He says he is entertaining some ideas, just entertaining them, not settling anything, not propounding any finalities. Give him free play, even on the highest levels.

He gets "up there," but it's not on a pillar. It is a "swinger of birches" that he dreams

> *of going back to be.*
> *It's when I'm weary of considerations,*
> *And life is too much like a pathless wood*
> *Where your face burns and tickles with the cobwebs*
> *Broken across it, and one eye is weeping*
> *From a twig's having lashed across it open.*

He would never climb on up into the inane, like an Indian fakir with a disappearing rope.

>   *He learned all there was*
> *To learn about not launching out too soon*
> *And so not carrying the tree away*
> *Clear to the ground. He always kept his poise*
> *To the top branches, climbing carefully*
> *With the same pains you use to fill a cup*
> *Up to the brim, and even above the brim.*
> *Then he flung outward, feet first, with a swish,*
> *Kicking his way down through the air to the ground.*

He frequently wants more "considerations." And he is constantly bringing himself down to earth. He defies gravity until he has it where it enables him to swing. He seems light while climbing. But in the swing down to the ground it is his substance that bends the birch and brings him back to "begin over."

What was a line between extremes is now a curve that nearly joins them. He has not occupied a middle point. He has not avoided extremes. He has touched both ends, butt and tip, and made them almost meet. He has seen many oppositions become almost unions. But "earth's the right place for love," and on earth things are dual; so he swings.

One evening before my fire he again considered the claims of monists. And finally he said, No, they never quite come to one. A great many things are like the flames there, in the fireplace. The outside margin on each side swings inward and upward, upward, almost to a point. It's as if they want to. Once in a great while the two sides of the blade of fire go so close to one that for an instant you aren't quite sure. But they lapse so quickly that you almost conclude you didn't see it one. And like all earthly things, they are two. Two here, with enough suggestion now and then of one to make the wishful say it is so now.

He has been called romantic, classic, realist; naturalist, humanist, defeatist, complaisant; radical, conservative, reactionary. He swings.

I am going to venture to give one brief example of his swinging. It will, I hope, illustrate his large inclusiveness, his quiet way of surpassing the prejudice that we all get to thinking of as boldly free from prejudice. It is a poem that has probably been misunderstood, "The Vanishing Red" from *Mountain Interval*. In 1911 Robert once remarked that one of his passions in boyhood was angry sympathy with the American Indians. But in 1917, when I read the concentrated blank verse poem, it shocked me. It seemed grimly sympathetic less with "the last Red Man in Acton" than with the Miller. He is said to have laughed when he came back from showing John the wheel pit.

THE VANISHING RED

He is said to have been the last Red Man
In Acton. And the Miller is said to have laughed—
If you like to call such a sound a laugh.
But he gave no one else a laugher's license.
For he turned suddenly grave as if to say,
'Whose business,—if I take it on myself,
Whose business—but why talk round the barn?—

When it's just that I hold with getting a thing done with.'
You can't get back and see it as he saw it.
It's too long a story to go into now.
You'd have to have been there and lived it.
Then you wouldn't have looked on it as just a matter
Of who began it between the two races.

Some guttural exclamation of surprise
The Red Man gave in poking about the mill
Over the great big thumping shuffling millstone
Disgusted the Miller physically as coming
From one who had no right to be heard from.
'Come, John,' he said, 'you want to see the wheel-pit?'

He took him down below a cramping rafter,
And showed him, through a manhole in the floor,
The water in desperate straits like frantic fish,
Salmon and sturgeon, lashing with their tails.
Then he shut down the trap door with a ring in it
That jangled even above the general noise,
And came upstairs alone—and gave that laugh,
And said something to a man with a meal-sack
That the man with the meal-sack didn't catch—then.
Oh, yes, he showed John the wheel-pit all right.

The man with the casual meal-sack intensifies the horror, as do the final words, "all right."

But Robert Frost has so patiently involved himself in the situation that now he feels something more than bare sympathy with the Indian. How about the redness after all—the wildness? Is it in the wheel pit? Is it, after all, the Indian? Or is the wildness in the way the Miller saw the Indian? He saw red. Does his laugh mean that now he has rid his world of ignorant, irrational wildness? Such elimination is always a violent and bloody process. The Miller is also uncomfortable, of course, laughing off his own feeling of guilt. What he has just done is more savage than anything the red man, John Indian, ever did. It is indeed more savage than most Indians ever were.

But Robert Frost sees the Miller's act *sub specie aeternitatis,* and that includes, I at last realized, the way that the Miller also saw it. He does, almost, "get back and see it as he saw it." And thus he has come to feel—along with the strong opposite feelings in sympathy with John—"disgusted physically" for the moment, as the Miller did, disgusted at the

> *guttural exclamation of surprise*
> *The Red Man gave in poking about the mill*
> *Over the great big thumping shuffling millstone.*

Robert has entered into, and so at long last understood, the exasperation that the Miller, a master at one of the basic mechanisms of civilization, feels when a creature of the wilds dares to comment on his precious mechanism with a grunt. Robert has contemplated till he pierced to the far-down place where all sorts of evil deeds have a kind of rightness. With no loss of his boyish sympathy with Indians he has transcended it. Now he feelingly understands that the Miller would not have been a good Miller if he had not believed with passion in his mechanized world.

He can no longer stare surprised because those who shared the Miller's civilization never did anything about the murder of the Indian. The Miller was a man of action who kept the order steady. And the Miller laughed.

Robert Frost was saying: Keep the wildness down; we have to; but if we keep it too completely down we shall discover it breaking out in us, ourselves.

VI

Up there, high enough

Robert Frost is always a little mocking toward witches (though he showed how much he liked them in "The Pauper Witch of Grafton," and how well he understood them). He never whirls with dervishes. Indeed, he once said he had "almost never experienced ecstasy."

But in 1945 he said that he lived most of the time in the state in which most people in the United States were the last few hours of election night: the state of wavering certainty. He was almost sure, but he was waiting until the decisive returns were in. That, of course, is why the feeling rises at the end of a poem, "Is that all?" It is also why so many readers come back to him as one who never, for all his guile, beguiled them.

> But naught extenuates or dims,
> Setting the thing that is supreme. (My emphasis.)

He won't give up common sense. He must have the practical, limited, everyday truth while he seeks the whole truth. Otherwise he would have only a magnificent illusion. He "cares so much for facts that he seems sometimes to care only for them."

He cares for concrete facts, not only for their color and shape and the drama of their action on one another, but also because he has so strong a faith in that which he has not—and no one has—grasped. He loves to see sharply because of the part of the whole truth that he can therefore see *in* what he sees. Concrete cases are containers. He comes down to cases—in the good American way—for themselves and, still more, for the implications they contain.

Rapture cannot snatch him clear away from the real; he keeps kicking down to earth. The ultimate real, which is what he has always wanted, must be attainable, if at all, in increasingly close relation with the particular real, this reality here at last fitted with all those other realities.

To discover the likenesses, to get the clear perception of relationships, he moves away and up. Once when young he spent three months alone on Ossipee Mountain finding out where he was and what he wanted, enough to keep on acting. He still keeps taking to the hills so that he can refuse offered choices between opposing goods. On the hills he can combine the good things, before he explores and adventures some more.

He mocks at all the statements of what experience turns out, in the last analysis, to be. He and I talked one night in 1928 of a new and highly successful book. The author had escaped from the throng, he said, and done a thing that varied from the intellectual and technical patterns of the time, which had become so tiresome. It had a rather nice beginning, he said, but a bad ending. In the end it said, Love is all. The man who remembers, Robert said, can't name one equivalent for *all*. The most a remembering man could say would be that this or that is all but all—all but.

Robert Frost is always showing that "the wire bands" on the oversimple name tags we so happily attach are being outgrown by the tree. If we leave them there, no fruit will ever grow; the wire will cut the cambium and kill the tree. "The philosopher values himself on the inconsistencies he can contain by main force," he wrote in 1936 in his Introduction to Sarah Cleghorn's autobiography, *Threescore*. "They are the two ends of a strut that keeps his mind from collapsing." But he went on: "He may take too much satisfaction in having once more remarked the two-endedness of things." He leaves his friends free to reject part of his wisdom, lets them piece together their torn formulas. He is only telling stories. If he helps us a little to start building "clear from the ground," it is incidentally.

For instance, thirty years ago he had helped me to grasp "the two-endedness of things" enough so that I could write for my first unpublished work, *Puritan Paradoxes*, a little essay that I called "Dealing with Dilemmas." It went something like this: In real life we are frequently all alone on a wide, wide prairie.

Only sun overhead and sand underfoot, with here and there a heap of tumbleweed against a section of old barbed-wire fence. Nothing in sight besides. Then all of a sudden appears a bull. Near you already, with tail aloft and bloodshot eyes, he roars at you and rushes. His horns are long and widely spaced. But they both point at you. One horn, you suddenly realize, is independence; the other is marriage. Or, no! One is loyalty to the group from whom you get your money; the other is loyalty to your own best perceptions. Or one is success in this world; the other is sticking to your guns. There are a myriad incompatible possibilities. And all seem to be about to disembowel you or to castrate. Which horn shall you let pierce you? As the bull lowers his head you suddenly have an access of blind nerve and common sense. You pivot and reach down and grasp both horns of the dilemma. And suddenly you are tossed, but not dislodged. And off you go, not picking your way, but alive and unhooked by both horns of the dilemma.

"Having ideas that are neither pro nor con," he wrote me in a letter in 1925, "is the happy thing. Get up there high enough and the differences that make controversy become only the two legs of a body, the weight of which is on one side in one period, on the other, in the next. Democracy monarchy; puritanism paganism; form and content; conservatism radicalism; systole diastole; rustic urbane; literary colloquial; work play. I should think too much of myself to let any teacher fool me into taking sides on any one of those oppositions. Maybe I'm wrong. But I was always wrong then. It's not just old age with me. I'm not like Maeldune weary of strife from having seen too much of it.—I've wanted to find some ways to transcend the strife method. I have found some. Mind you I'd fight a healthy amount. This is no pacifism. It is not so much anti-conflict as it is something beyond conflict—such as poetry and religion that is not just theological dialectic. I'll bet I could tell of spiritual realizations that for a moment at least would overawe the contentious."

Up there high enough to find ways to transcend and to have spiritual realizations, but still only as high as he could climb, still longing more than claiming, he has sufficient wholeness to stay separate and to continue one among the many.

VII

He could love the things he
loves for what they are

Robert Frost was "out for stars," but he couldn't
close his ears to thrush music "Far in the pillared
dark." One of his "wishes," long before his first book,
was to "steal away" into some "vastness" that
"stretched away unto the edge of doom." There he
could be "more sure." He soon stopped asking for
such sureness. Even in the early poem uttering his
craving for the utterly uttermost, the line that in 1911
he ran his finger proudly along was,

Or highway where the slow wheel pours the sand.

He has stayed not very far from the highway since
and never lingered too long in "the place of standing
still."

He knew the way "Thought cleaves the interstellar
gloom," but he was always drawn back by love, which
"has earth to which she clings." As for him, being

masculine, he has moved in both directions, "toward heaven" and "To Earthward." He has therefore never deceptively satisfied his own or his reader's craving for universality. He has swung birches. And he has swung a scythe. There are truths in "Mowing" that most criticism ignores.

His love for things and for a person never gets entirely free from his love for truth.

Anything more than the truth would have seemed
*   too weak*
To the earnest love . . . .

Anything less than the truth has a ring of the brave and the honest. But most of us catch ourselves attributing a little that is not at present there, in order to keep on loving. That "anything more" should be scrupulously avoided is a strange thought. It recurs constantly in the poems of Robert Frost, and it means that the truth itself, bare and exact, is so good, to one who sees it fully, or so much preferable to any misguided efforts of wishers, at worst, that any literary enhancement is a violation. He likes—and loves—the actual, and when he uses it he will not at all distort it. That is Robert Frost—for better or for worse; anything "more" is vulgar and cheap. But if you are inclined to turn from the actual pasture meadow to what might be there if—then you have a craving that Robert Frost has evidently seen beyond.

Always "against a divided life," Robert Frost has none of the inverted sentimentality that is given off by denied or belittled emotions. None of his has been shut up in a cyst. None has lurked concealed to burst in silliness. Sweetness has not turned sour nor bitterness insipid. He could say in "To Earthward":

> *Love at the lips was touch*
> *As sweet as I could bear;*
> *And once that seemed too much;*
> *I lived on air*
>
> *That crossed me from sweet things*
> *The flow of—was it musk*
> *From hidden grapevine springs*
> *Down hill at dusk?*
>
> *I had the swirl and ache*
> *From sprays of honeysuckle*
> *That when they're gathered shake*
> *Dew on the knuckle.*
>
> *I craved strong sweets, but those*
> *Seemed strong when I was young;*
> *The petal of the rose*
> *It was that stung.*

His feelings have matured. He has not outgrown them. He grew with them. He digested and composed the incident sufferings, so that

> *Now no joy but lacks salt*
> *That is not dashed with pain*

And weariness and fault;
I crave the stain

Of tears, the aftermark
Of almost too much love,
The sweet of bitter bark
And burning clove.

A hasty thinker might exclaim at this point: "Well, he evidently was very lucky in love." But while he doubtless was lucky, and in ways unlucky, the point is not his luck. The point is that one who "loves the things he loves for what they are" is deserving of more than most of us deserve.

He cares if he notices. His kind of objectivity is not that achieved by inspecting objects as they would appear if he lacked emotion.

Always he has a mischievous realization that

We dance round in a ring and suppose,
But the Secret sits in the middle and knows.

He cherishes no ideal image of what person, bird, or brook should be. He is, therefore, hospitable to discrepancies. He welcomes variations. He continues to look, long after he sees what to call a thing, and often finds something to love. If the actual brook has dried up he keeps looking and takes notice of the

jewel-weed,
Weak foliage that is blown upon and bent

Even against the way its waters went.
Its bed is left a faded paper sheet
Of dead leaves stuck together by the heat—
A brook to none but who remember long.

Robert Frost has made good on the claim he made in "Hyla Brook,"

We love the things we love for what they are.

VIII

Yet he had fears, too

What, though, gave him the force? The courage? The guts? I don't know.

He felt in early years the vast indifference of the universe. More congealing it was to the flow of impulse than cruelty or contempt:

> *And yet with neither love nor hate,*
> *Those stars like some snow-white*
> *Minerva's snow-white marble eyes*
> *Without the gift of sight.*

He knew what it was to be surprised, when "running with joy," by the sudden sound of the demiurge's laugh,

> *As of one who utterly couldn't care.*

And so I could say that his refusal of the usual security deceptions was made possible by despair. I could say that the force is the force of rapture. If you have known the top of joy, the quicksands of dejection cannot quite suck you under. The memory of delight will not allow you

> *To go with the drift of things,*
> *To yield with a grace to reason.*

"Rose Pogonias" is one of many poems that show this deep delight. But what makes possible such absolute delight? It is rare and difficult.

Aware of tragedy, and knowing the feelings of those who are defeated, Robert Frost is not indifferent to doubts about the worth of the human enterprise. He has often heard "A Question," whether "the soul-and-body scars/Were not too much to pay for birth."

He plunged to the depths, contemplated despair, and came back believing that we are and always can be like the white counterwave in "West-Running Brook," "not gaining but not losing." It pleased him to watch it,

> *unresisted,*
> *Save by some strange resistance in itself,*
> *Not just a swerving, but a throwing back,*
> *As if regret were in it and were sacred.*

IX

He takes his risks "assertively"

Where so great a daring and so great a delicacy of balance are required, delegation and compromise do not work. And so Robert Frost is ironically "Assertive."

> *Let me be the one*
> *To do what is done.*

All but slaves have some place where they not only set foot but put their foot down; all but those who fit his pitying description, "A decent product of life's ironing out."

But such quiet rascals determined to "make the least difference even the slightest" none the less have their fears. (Robert Frost talks, writes, and acts as if the number of quiet rascals is potentially great. He thinks the United States is and must continue the most favorable land for them to flourish in. He implies that "our kind" or "my kind" are numerous. And it is funny-sad to hear him reluctantly admit that, where he then happens to be, many are "the other kind.")

He is always sticking his foot in the closing doors of systems to keep his chance to be "the one." Let us preserve some insecurity, he says.

"Two fears," he wrote in 1935 in his Introduction to Edwin Arlington Robinson's *King Jasper*, "two fears should follow us through life. There is the fear that we shan't prove worthy in the eyes of someone who knows us at least as well as we know ourselves. That is the fear of God. And there is the fear of Man —the fear that men won't understand us and we shall be cut off from them."

In 1947 two poems in *Steeple Bush* were "The Fear of God" and "The Fear of Man," and *A Masque of Mercy* again gave form to the religious fear:

PAUL
Yes, there you have it at the root of things.
We have to stay afraid deep in our souls
Our sacrifice, the best we have to offer,
And not our worst nor second best, our best,
Our very best, our lives laid down like Jonah's,
Our lives laid down in war and peace, may not
Be found acceptable in Heaven's sight.
And that they may be is the only prayer
Worth praying. May my sacrifice
Be found acceptable in Heaven's sight.
KEEPER
Let the lost millions pray it in the dark!
My failure is no different from Jonah's.

We both have lacked the courage in the heart
To overcome the fear within the soul
And go ahead to any accomplishment.
Courage is what it takes and takes the more of
Because the deeper fear is so eternal.

But if Robert Frost has been swinging from delight to wisdom beset by those two fears all his life, why isn't he dully earnest?

X

Because it's a funny world

"It's a funny world." If he said it once, he has said it a thousand times. "It's a funny world." He said it sadly, he said it mockingly, he said it calmly as he slowly shook his head at the solemn explanations of great minds, and he said it smiling as he made an opening for more truth. Even when he sighs you feel that under all his warm commiseration, all his anger, all his unshed tears at "unavenged injustices," lurks a mad-gladness that he can surely count on this continuing "a funny world."

It is all funny, and it's always funny, and if anyone ever thinks he settles anything so that the funniness is gone, that is the best of all occasions for a smile.

Seriously it's funny. It's seriously funny. And it's funny because it's serious. You often have to wait a while before you are amused. And even then most good smiles have a disappearing trace at least of rue-fulness. Some of his have had, rather, but a trace, though unmistakable, of mirth—as when he told me recently the saddest irony he ever told, lately discovered in his own life.

Not to attempt a chart of funniness, since it has its being in small shifts that spoil the correspondence of the clearly known "fact" with reality—

> *What now is inland shall be ocean isle,*
> *Then eddies playing round a sunken reef*
> *Like the curl at the corner of a smile;*

—this is a way I have seen the world as funny, as I got over bafflement following long talks with Robert.

Between "I s'pose" and "I d'know" he is always drawing up his heavy eyebrows and showing more causes for the event you had explained. Their relation is never merely temporal. The tail he shows you is in the mouth. The roots are overhead. History depends on dubious prophecy. Afterwards is, though inconceivably, a shaper of the present, and the present past. And we move towards what is far behind. The contents include the container (as each man makes his own world and is at the center of it, yet has it within him; as all of our family that we have experienced is inside our minds, and yet each of us, mind and all, is part of that family). The parts are containers of the whole. Yet the whole is more than all the parts in sum. And if we expand to embrace the all, we pop like a soap bubble; a thin round flake of dirt dries against the wall. It's a funny world, you for the moment agree.

But I'm not saying that Robert Frost philosophized himself into humor. I had rather say that he averted the aberrations of the philosopher because he always knew and never for long forgot that it is a funny world. And to the annoyance of that in philosophers which craves some absolute dependence, Robert Frost has, willingly, some of the shift in himself. When we are intensely earnest because we feel our firm foundations slipping he looks shifty. He won't be pinned down. He does not maintain a balance; he keeps gaining one. He throws his weight not where the weight of opinion, considered and authoritative opinion, rests, but where realities are that opinion has of late ignored.

Back in the winter of 1917 when the alert of mind in America were unanimously denouncing the Bolshevist revolution, he was the only person I encountered who thought we had better give the Russians the benefit of the doubt a while longer. In 1938 when so many liberals were defending the suspension of freedom and redefining democracy to provide for dictatorship, he was quietly questioning their faith. When young poets by the score were discovering Donne and Gerard Manley Hopkins, and all the English majors had found out that Longfellow was sentimental and silly, Robert Frost was reading in public poems by Longfellow that most of us had never noticed and pointing out the drama in them, the wisdom, the play, and the skilled and accurate rhythms. Before anyone had heard of John Dewey outside the University of Chicago and Columbia, Robert Frost was mocking at the rigidities and unrealities of formal education, turning his back on them, and then, as teacher, inconspicuously sabotaging them in academy and normal school. But by the time that all the quick catchers-on were practicing the new progressive stereotypes, Robert Frost was saying school was a place for drill, rote learning, the three R's; literature and experience were too delicate and too much alive for school. Let school deal with numbers and letters. Let it not mechanically meddle with imagination, insight, taste.

When you come around to agreeing with Robert Frost he does not agree with you. I never knew that to fail. He says "That's right," and he quotes corroboratingly something that you said a while ago; then he tells a funny incident that backs you up. But, no, it always has a turn. He is always turning tables, showing that someone had forgotten that all tables have under sides.

XI

The mischief in him is often gay

The mischief is usually in him. Summer, fall, and winter, not only spring. Whatever it is you talk about, there's sooner or later something funny about it, though often your smile won't come or is constrained. And if you are put off your balance by his rectification of the balance, you can see him as perverse, irrational, a fool.

He gives you the chance to save your face, if you refrain from saying so, saving his. If you laugh and half your laugh is at him, and only half with him, that is all right. He knows that he is funny, too. He could not stay friendly, otherwise, with the funny world. But the thing is that, without resignation, he has accepted the funny world. No matter how much he laughs at you, he laughs with you, too, at the same time.

The joke is on him, also. It is in him, too. For he has taken much of the mischief within. And I mean the cruel mischief, too. The topsy-turvy mischief and the mortal mischief, both. He meant it when he wrote, in his *Masque of Reason,* slyly and seriously attributing the words to God:

> *the discipline man needed most*
> *Was to learn his submission to unreason ...*

A very different thing from submission to reason, and with opposite results.

In this funny world submitting to reason is giving up Job's stubborn faith. Though he had, he said, to "let" God "off"

> *From telling me Your reason, don't assume*
> *I thought You had none. Somewhere back*
> *I knew You had one. But this isn't it*
>
> . . . .
>
> *I'd give more for one least beforehand reason*
> *Than all the justifying ex-post-facto*
> *Excuses trumped up ....*

Robert Frost knows reasons, and good ones, that he has belief in, but individually and collectively they are not sufficient:

> *what I get*
> *Is almost less than I can understand.*
> *But I don't mind. Let's leave it as it stood.*
> *The point was it was none of my concern.*

And even the best reason leaves Robert Frost, like his Job, "thinking of the Devil" and declaring

We can't leave him out.

The mischief is what saves us from giving in to reason, what keeps us, if anything keeps us, humorous and imaginative, willing to gamble on our own designs made as we go along, and ready to commit ourselves despite error that no patience can avoid, believing a little beyond reason.

Robert Frost's irony appears in his treatment of necessity. Necessity is central to his thinking, and his way of thinking about it is always being misunderstood. I shall never forget the protest an able and learned professor burst out with in 1920 in connection with Robert Frost's lines in " 'Out, Out—' "

And they, since they
Were not the one dead, turned to their affairs.

My friend said the ending spoiled an otherwise good poem.

A few things, such as an event that has already happened, there is nothing much to do about. We can only muster fortitude to accept. There can be no paltering with the past. "No more to build on there."

But you have to think more than twice before you "accept the inevitable." I recall the relaxed irony in Robert Frost's voice when I divulged in 1924 that I was learning to accept the inevitable. "If you could tell what *is* inevitable," he said.

XII

In teaching he would protect
the students from the institution

At least twice and at least ten years apart Robert Frost told interviewers that he must be just an ordinary man. He may have teased Henry Wallace about his idealization of the common man. He may have angrily called a dean who had let slip a real teacher a "commonordinarian." But he "would not be taken as ever having rebelled." He would be nothing less than an ordinary man, always "more than half" there, always, if possible, all there. Most of his difference consisted in having given up less than usual of normal human sensibilities and desires. He composed a character with what he kept.

His mischief was never a mask. It is a native sparkle that he continually rekindles in his persistent seeking for the center; his steel strikes the necessary flint as he willfully indulges his craving for "the highest reaches."

"Being alive is a lot of fun" to the last if something has not gone wrong. And being funny is not very peculiar in a funny world. There ought to be ways for more and more of us to keep up the systole and diastole, the expansion and contraction, the breathless swing from the crude subject matter of experience to form. And so, no matter what the differences between himself and other people, he has wanted to keep regaining touch. He has wanted to win the affection of many of his fellows and, holding fast to all that really matters, with no crowding and no infringement, to show them how to have ideas. Then he would pay them the compliment of withdrawing: "give him that terribly abandoned feeling, left to the horrors of his own thought and conscience."

He has not let out all the cats in his bag, but in the midst of his career he said: "The lack of ideas in young minds is shocking to me. That's my quarrel with everybody I know. I want you putting two and two together, and I don't care a hoorah for anything else. That's my interest. As long as I stay around the colleges that will be my reason for staying. I have run away, you know. I ran away twice and I walked away a good many times. You see I haven't time to tell you all the devices that I use, the attitudes I strike, to convince people that I mean that.

". . . the weakness, the strength, to be swept away, to be carried away, by something more than beer, and games, and so on. I want everybody to be carried away by something. I'd rather it would be beer and games than nothing, I think. I like people who can't help thinking and talking about things to the highest reaches. That of course is the great thing.

"You may say there's plenty of provision for that in school. But is there? Freedom to do more than you're asked to do. No you haven't either. Every minute's provided for. I would say to my class, 'I'm entitled to nine hours of your time—three in class and two outside for each of those. All right, I present it to you. This is the time you can lose yourselves. You've got to do some losing of yourself to find yourself. "I touch it and remit it," as Kipling says. I'll keep the institution off your back to that extent.

" 'Nothing may happen in nine weeks out of ten. All those hours may be wasted. I think in the years, though, something may happen. Let it stand for a kind of gravestone for what you didn't do.' "

That is sabotage. It arises from sympathy with a good mind, not yet subdued to docility, nor scared to the practical pretense of it. Reverence and passionate sympathy blend in Robert Frost's mischief-making.

Education, in his sense of it, is like his kind of funny world. It declines to make a shut-eye assumption that there is "any universal reason" in man's possession or about to be. Robert Frost indignantly denounced college teaching that "frisks Freshmen of their principles." At Bread Loaf in 1925 he declared that a boy with all his beliefs drawn out of him is in no condition to learn. Or even to live. Everybody needs some beliefs as unquestionable as the axioms of geometry. No postulates deliberately adopted could ever have the force. We had to have unarguable, undemonstrable, unmistakable axioms, just three or four. And if we didn't abuse our minds we should surely have them. One such is that genuineness is better than pretense. Another is that meanness is intolerable in oneself. And another is that death is better than being untrustworthy.

Robert Frost's kind of education accepts, with Job, the realization that though reason "is what we're most concerned with," in "the trial by existence" it is

> *of the essence of the trial*
> *You shouldn't understand it at the time.*
> *It had to seem unmeaning to have meaning.*

Something should save the students from thinking they can be given the answer. They must learn that there is no way to get out of suffering. They must personally and passionately realize what Robert Frost was once more realizing when he wrote "In Hardwood Groves." Not as a fact only must going "down into the dark decayed" be known; it must be emotionally known; it must be seen as tragic beauty.

Something in school days should save us from being "too ready to believe the most," from the cowardly modesty of the "literate farmer," who thought there was

> *"No need for us to rack our common heads."*

Something in school should save us from the fatal credulity of progress prophets. Something should save the students from supposing that the way of intelligence is eliminating opposition and waste. Something must be present in education to remind them that as lying down goes with love, so waste goes with growth and opposition with night and day.

One time when Robert Frost was talking of how we are fooled by thinking of things as continuous and unbroken, he said: "Sleep is probably a symbol of the interruption, the disconnection that I want in life. Your whole life can be so logical that it seems to me like a ball of hairs in the stomach of an angora cat. It should be broken up and interrupted, and then brought together by likeness, free likeness."

XIII

But keep the generalizations broad and loose

His very posture was symbolic as he talked large and loose, one night by the side of his huge stone fireplace at South Shaftsbury: slumped way down in his big chair, with spread legs stretching forth his comfortable old-fashioned shoes. His mind moved swift and far; his words came measured though in play. Now and then his broad, hairy fingers rubbed around the blunt tip of his nose, and now and then they deliberatively mussed his graying hair.

Metaphors, he said, try "to say matter in terms of spirit, or spirit in terms of matter—to make the final unity." That is "the greatest of all attempts, the greatest attempt that ever failed. We stop just short there. But it is the height of poetry, the height of all thinking, the height of all poetic thinking, that attempt to say matter in terms of spirit and spirit in terms of matter."

Between the spiritual and the material are shades of difference, but not absolute clear distinctions. You've seen, he said, a stream of water of one color flowing into a stream of another color. The marginal line between them sways with the current and the season.

That swaying of the margin makes it impossible, he said, to refine precisely on any general ideas about life. That's why broad statements of wisdom are truer, when you want them to apply to more than a single particular case—nearer true than elaborately qualified formulations. They don't exactly coincide with the swaying marginal line, but they are near enough. The Ten Commandments are near enough, he said. We try for closeness to the swaying line. But since it sways, when we are general we can no more than approximate it.

It is like that with law and justice. It has to be rough—rough justice. But we achieve approximation. You realize it, he said, when you compare the imperfect justice of the courts with that outside the law. The punishment of the gangster who double-crosses a pal is more arbitrary and merciless than that of any court. And there isn't any jury. Punishment pursues him clear across the world, and it never lapses until the double-crosser is rubbed out. We had better keep the general general, and when it comes to cases of our own size be as particular as we can.

XIV

And get students to start performing

Long before he was a celebrity Robert Frost used to say that he could never plan an hour with a class. On the way to class he thought of something to serve as nucleus, and usually, before the closing bell, he and the class had brought something to a shape.

"The best hour I ever had in the classroom," he once said, "was good only for the shape it took. I like an encounter to shape up, unifying however roughly. There is such a thing as random talk, but it is to be valued as scouting for coinable gold."

He doesn't have it in him to lecture three times a week, he says, sixty-odd times a year. "I refuse," he says, "to stand up and lecture a steady stream for fear of the consequences to my character. . . . Three days a week . . . is three times as much as I have the patience to face the audience [that] has been doing nothing to help itself in the intervals."

When he does lecture he doesn't confine himself to alleged facts and the opinions of opposed authorities. He doesn't leave his hearers in the dark about his personal judgment. He never could have said what one brilliant teacher said and thousands may have thought: "What would happen to the students if they knew what we really thought?" It is true that most who hear Robert Frost do not know what he thinks. But that is not because he does not commit himself. That is not because he doesn't try to make his utterances as clear as fidelity to truth permits. It is because his thoughts are not detachable from a life. No other man can think them before he has had the experiences and made the decisions. What good listeners get from listening to him is not opinions they can accept or reject; what they get, even from lectures, is an experience. It may cause thoughts to dawn on them.

But he never acts surprised at small effects. He meant his epigram, "Great events yield all but imperceptible effects." His purpose in teaching, to evoke an "answer from within" the student, to "get where he lives, among his realities," could only be effected lightly. He knew the contradictions, the ambiguities, too well to expect immediate or large or numerous successes in getting people to put this and that together. Irony tones his enthusiasm. His sympathy gives reticence to his energy. He does what he does with glancing touch.

He cares what is going on in those he talks with. He uses memories of all his old past feelings to put himself in the place of one who squirms, or brightens too soon or too much, or suddenly straightens his mouth, or thrusts out a foot or an underlip. But the end at which his effort of understanding aims is standing the student on his own head. He uses many devices to get anyone with "inclinations" he "could call" his "own" to start performing. But he does it as if "not much concerned." There is more at stake than anyone must be aware of.

"But don't let them ever hear you use the word 'response,' " he once said. In his desire for people who are not looking "to be told what to think and what to do," for people "who have marked wide horizons for themselves," he has disciplined himself not to get forbiddingly intense. He does not forget that

> *Things must expect to come in front of us*
> *A many times.*

And he has always been "lazy." He would rather see time go to waste than give anyone "too much world at once." He would wait for a few to get something "at heart." He saw no need for more people educated as the professor was in "A Hundred Collars," to be democratic only "on principle." He would wait to bring out a little "the lines" that were "native to the grain." He would not ask questions to which he knew the answers, and foster the perennial schoolboy mentality that recalls facts "in the order learned." He would encourage those who, gaining knowledge through desire, had "taken impressions freely before [they had] any notion of their use."

Their knowledge is the opposite of "stuffing." He wants no part in the increase of stuffed selves. "The latest modern stuffing," he said, "is no more fruitful than reactionary stuffing." A stuffed shirt is blown up with what is not digested; a stuffed shirt "doesn't care what he thinks of himself, provided the world thinks well."

He gets some amusement from "all kinds of people," since it is "all kinds of a world," but, for his part, he looks for a few more like the boy in "The Death of the Hired Man" who studied "Latin like the violin because he liked it," a few more who think of college as "a place for gentlemen to be self-made," a few more who have found out a lot of things that most others do not know and can suggest ideas to each other. "It is the essence of symposiums I'm after. Heaps of ideas and the subject matter of books purely incidental. Rooms full of students who want to talk and talk and spill out ideas, and suggest things to me I never thought of. It is like the heaping up of all the children's hands, all the family's hands, on the parental knee, in the game we used to play by the fireside."

He keeps trying for such "polite conversation" in which no one took anyone too seriously, but real desires would rise, cross, check, oppose—in which feelings really play, and all come toward a joining, and so suggest a happier orchestration of the incompatible roars and screams, sighs and chuckles.

XV

With the freedom of their materials

"Doubts of laid-on education" set Robert Frost free
for the real thing. "Our minds," he said in a letter in
1920, "are so crowded with what we have been told
to look for that they have no room for accidental discoveries." But from the time he graduated valedictor-
ian from Lawrence High School, he "would not have
it so." He would not crowd or be crowded, mentally
or any other way. And so he has taught, with patient
use of accident, to promote discoveries.

Before he won the ambiguous privilege of fame he
taught high school kids, intending teachers, and once,
early, when he was helping in his mother's school, big
toughs he had first to subdue by force. He did not gain
his educational insights among the exceptional.

But he is alert to "recognize Mind when" he meets
"with it in any guise." He has met with considerable
specks oftener than the devisers of textbooks and the

conductors of organized courses. Unlike them, he is frankly impatient with "slaves" or "sheep"—those averse to freedom.

At Pinkerton Academy, where he taught thirty-five hours a week for years, as well as at Dartmouth College, where in 1950 he met a few picked and voluntary students once a week for three hours, he tried "to give—the freedom I'd like to have."

If only a very few know what to make of freedom, or exactly enjoy such superlative responsibility, he smiles, tells another astonishingly relevant incident from ancient history, or recites a modern-seeming seventeenth-century poem.

At Pinkerton his first act was to dump a lot of dull books about vocations that a practical-minded English teacher had preferred to literature. He ignored composition texts, too. And, instead, he got the kids to reading aloud and hearing him read many poems from Palgrave's *Golden Treasury*. And he read with them stories like Mark Twain's "Jumping Frog," with its hilarious warning—which Robert didn't let them miss—about how you may lose your spring, H. G. Wells's "Country of the Blind," Stevenson's "Bottle Imp," and Hawthorne's "Mr. Higginbotham's Catastrophe."

Being friendly, he broke the dismal spell that holds kids back from a natural experience. His own amusement and pleasure were on the side of play, not on the side of calculated benefit; and the kids were infected. They began to sense and feel the experiences in the poems and stories—just so long as it was fun and maybe a trifle improper, as compared with diagraming and writing out corrections. They even came to enjoy and ponder the implications, exchanging, now and then, a quick, conspiratorial glance with the tall man in comfortable unpressed clothes who didn't act the least bit like a teacher.

He showed them that what makes a story of a story is "the turn," "the twist," "the wiggle, at least." And they began to learn about form. The point with the stories and, as much, with Milton's "Lycidas," for instance, was not to have read celebrated authors, but to see and to be pleased.

He got them to limber up their humor and to imagine, bodily and all. He unostentatiously asked them to do *The Importance of Being Ernest, The School for Scandal,* and Milton's *Comus.* And he got real performances. All they needed to know—came to want to know—about eighteenth-century society and the world of Oscar Wilde they picked up on the side. For *Comus* they hired animal masks for the rout. The chairman of the school board volunteered to get them the use of the silver communion service for the magic banquet. The cast was too young to be self-conscious about the poetry or the author. And the paying audience gave every indication of unsophisticated entertainment. In all three plays they aimed at nothing short of the real thing.

Always the one insistence was, as Robert wrote me, by way of rare advice, about fifteen years after his days at Derry, "Make it real." When the institution that employed him, which he was "willing to let pretty

much alone," insisted on something unreal he burlesqued it. He told his Pinkerton debaters when they
had a good idea to ascribe it to Daniel Webster or
George Washington: judges, he told them, would find
their thoughts convincing only when masquerading as
not their own. When a prize contest for an oration was
required, he let the ten eligible boys each write something. When they handed in what they had written he
suggested an improved sentence or two. They revised
and handed in again. The same process was repeated
with a different part of the oration. And so on, again
and again, until at last—the way Robert tells it—in
the long series of revisions all of the boys' balderdash
had been replaced by substitutions, written dramatic-
ally, in character, by Robert Frost. The ten boys
memorized the orations. Finally he was also called
upon to select the winner. The donor expressed amaze-
ment at the excellence and naturalness of the ten
orators.

He would not assign topics, at Pinkerton or anywhere. He advised his pupils, there, to find something
"common to experience but uncommon to expression."
Could one of them, for instance, make him see pigeons
on the street: their primly placed lavender feet, their
iridescent necks, the way they poked their heads in
walking, and the dainty way they picked out a grain
of oats?—something as little looked at but familiar as
that.

When they had a flash of genuine observation and
imprisoned the sight without a trace of literary cant,
he was pleased and let them know it. "Praise them in

the absolute or not at all," he used to say. If he couldn't praise he kept quiet.

He was no early Dewey. Freedom from rote learning was not his point; there was need for that. It was not freedom from direction, as in those tutorial courses where there is "nothing to think about." It was not freedom from lecturing, with the teacher prodding from behind, or snapping a finger on the student's head and exhorting, "Think, now, think." It wasn't freedom to "say, 'No, no, no' to the teacher's 'Yes, yes, yes.' I always shrink in good company from contradiction," he said. The freedom he patiently sought to give was "The freedom *of* something—freedom of the city, or the freedom of your subject. I might mean expertness! . . . I'd just as soon you'd go off sideways from anything I've said," or anything read in class. "Go off at a tangent. That's a kind of freedom I should like to encourage in my class. But I can't do exactly that—I can only make provision for it in my manner."

Robert Frost seems always to have known what the disproportionately instructed never realize: that the materials of which a good mind achieves the freedom are always a different set for each person. He always had the courage to think into an order all his own. He knew that the best frames of reference can but ignore shades and characteristics of any single person's potential truth. He has been accurately acquainted with plenty of the frames of reference, as they replaced each other in history and in his own lifetime. But he has kept serenely on, spinning his own wisdom at home. Prefabricated wisdom, he saw, is roughly adequate only for that single person who once wove and spun the initial fabric, in the awkward freedom of his private mind. Even that spinner would outgrow his web if he kept on living, and would have to eat and digest segments and spin them more inclusively. One who craves to be wise—as distinguished from learned or mechanically intellectual—must achieve his own homemade freedom.

And so Robert Frost's teaching patiently attempted the very thing that "To the Right Person" his poems generally accomplish. At Pinkerton Academy, at Plymouth Normal School, at Amherst, at Michigan, at Bread Loaf, at Harvard, at Yale, at the New School, at Dartmouth, and at all the many colleges where he held his "polite conversations," Robert Frost's teaching is giving people the freedom of their own imaginations.

XVI

Tempting them to be daringly good

You can do what is subtly demanded of you; or you can do more and better than is demanded. It may have been in that meditative quarter year in a house by himself on Ossipee Mountain that Robert Frost decided that. If you take the second way, you must expect for a long time to be taken for a somewhat suspicious character. He was prepared to be "left . . . to the way" he "took." He was "prepared for rage." And he never held others to blame; he never expected pity; he never pitied himself.

But he finds it fun to be close to danger.

> *The danger not an inch outside*
> *Behind the porthole's slab of glass*
> *And double ring of fitted brass*
> *I trust feels properly defied.*

He told with gloating of his reply to an anxious

parent at Derry who wanted to know if her son was reading the books required for entrance to M. I. T. Her son had better see to it, he said. He didn't know. He wasn't, he implied, concerned with requirements. He was concerned with the boy's learning to read, really read; if the boy learned, he could, soon enough, read by himself any required books or authors. And the class went right on reading plays and stories and great poems.

Perversely he wanted all he took an interest in to have a similar audacity. In 1929 a brilliant young instructor who had been studying in Harvard Graduate School spoke of going to Oxford.

"Why not Madrid?" said Robert. "Or Bogotá?" He looked at the young man quizzically. "Find out something that the gang don't know." And then, continuing in his gentle, subtly sympathetic way: "The main thing, after all, though, of course, is not so much to have a place of your own to bring discoveries from; the main thing is to have a place in the mind. What we need to get is a world of our own."

At Bread Loaf in the summer of 1924 he told a little theater full of high school English teachers: An English teacher has three prime duties. He would state them, he said, in the order of their importance. The English teacher's first duty is to himself—then, with a questioning smile, herself. Her first duty is to herself. Her second duty is to the books. Her third duty is to her students.

The bright and shallow ones forced a cackle and dismissed his paradox as "humor." The humorous ones thought freshly. Good teaching, they saw he meant, requires first of all good teachers: blithe and winsome persons, persons who can establish contact between the subject matter and the girl or boy they teach. They must not be fagged or cowed or flustered. They might better throw away a bunch of themes. They mustn't come to class with a conscientious headache. The bright ones got the drift.

Another time when he issued a challenge was when, by way of final examination, he put on the blackboard at the end of his course in "Neglected Writers" at Amherst: "Do something."

Some of the boys got up and left as soon as he was upstairs in his office. Others climbed the stairs, knocked, and told him "how much" they had "got out of the course." Others crammed two bluebooks with all they could recall of what they thought he had said. One or two collected themselves and wrote a thoughtful paragraph, or recounted vividly an incident that embodied the most memorable philosophical discovery that they had made during the previous months. With them he had succeeded. The others were as they were at the end of usual courses; except that even they had had an unusual exposure. Years later one of them might see.

One commencement, near the end of Robert Frost's second stretch at Amherst, President King was apparently pleased with what Robert Frost had said in his address—or with the state of mind just then of his trustees—for the President said to the poet that he would like him to ask for an administrative favor.

"Even to the half of thy kingdom?" Robert said.

"Even to the half of my kingdom," President King smilingly replied.

Robert asked for a scholarship to be given to a student of his selection, according to provisions that he set. The president agreed. And Robert selected the boy who had shown the most power of making up his own mind, and stipulated that he should "go somewhere in the United States," take no courses, seek no guidance, and produce something to suit himself. Neither project nor production had to be submitted. He was to be terrifyingly on his own.

Always Robert Frost's test of education was: Did it develop and equip the ability to go it on your own? The good teacher, he once said, "knows how to get more out of a student by surrounding him with an atmosphere of expectation than by putting the screws on him. The sort of teacher who will reverse the whole relationship between student and teacher as it has been, who will encourage the student to make his own trouble without waiting for his teacher to make it for him, who will turn the teacher's claim on the student into the student's claim on the teacher. . . . Courses should be a means of introduction, to give the students a claim on me, so that they may come to me at any time, outside of class periods."

But "having a claim on" him was quite another matter than "using your teacher," a shibboleth the so-to-say talented boys picked up from some faculty member during an earlier administration at Amherst. He burlesqued that idea they seemed proud of having

· 67

swallowed whole, one day in class, by laying his leg along the desk and saying, "Use me." No one proceeded to pull his leg.

What he meant was genuine human give-and-take. "All teaching," he said, "could be based on informal contacts." He would like to see it tried so, in "research laboratory, studio apprenticeship, and the salon of good minds. . . . Some" teachers, he said, "I'd give less. Some I'd give—isn't there a phrase, 'Nothing else but'?"

In such a better than standard college, "The business of the teacher is, I presume," he said, "to challenge the student's purpose. 'This is life, your career is ahead of you,' he must say. 'Now what are you going to do about it?' I do not mean that the challenge should be made in words. That, I should think, is nearly fruitless. . . . No, what I mean is that his life must say that, his own work must say that.

"If a teacher is evidently a power outside as well as inside the college, one of whom you can hear along other highways, then the teacher is of deep potential value to the student. . . . I have always thought a man's chief strength came from being able to say (after Paul and Kipling) 'Of no mean city am I—of no mean college am I—speaking intellectually.' For my part I am helped by the thought of the artists who are my fellow citizens. It is encouraging to belong to the same circle with people who see life large."

In every college that Robert Frost has done his inconspicuous best to make "no mean college," he has been deftly and gently working toward a condition in which students could demonstrate the quality of their academic acquirement not chiefly by examinations but "by performance." If they were students of science and they—as does happen, though all too rarely—contributed to an important discovery, that would be their demonstration. If they were students of history, anthropology, philosophy, or literature in any language, "they could come and talk, they could express themselves in the publications on the Campus, or they could write elsewhere." The sort of teacher he was and the sort he was looking for could not be fooled by mere compilation and disguised reiteration. It would be his to judge.

"I have never complained of having had to mark," he said. "I had rather mark anyone for anything—for his looks, his carriage, his ideas, his correctness, his exactness, anything you please—I would rather give him a mark in terms of letters, A, B, C, D, than have to use adjectives on him. We are all being marked by each other all the time, classified, ranked, put in our place, and I see no escape from that. I am no sentimentalist. You have got to mark, first of all, for accuracy, for correctness. But if I am going to give a mark, that is the least part of my marking. The hard part is the part beyond that, the part where the adventure begins."

To teach much better than is expected, to be daringly good, "two minimal things, . . . taste and judgment," must be appraised, and also "imagination, initiative, enthusiasm, inspiration and originality—dread words."

XVII

*And trying to see how close to books
he could bring them*

"The nearest thing in college to the arts is not the classroom," Robert Frost said with the emphasis of irritation, in 1933 on the way to Rutland after receiving the doctorate of letters at the first college he had "run away from." "The nearest thing to the arts is the gymnasium and the athletic field."

Your heart is fully in it. You excel at tennis, vaulting, tumbling, racing, or any kind of ball game because you have the art to put all you've got into it. You're completely alert. You're hotly competitive and yet a good sport. You're having fun, skillfully taking risks, increasing the hazards. Putting up the bar in the high jump, for instance. You deliberately limit yourself by traditional, artificial rules. What you try for is effective and appropriate form. And success is measured by surpassing performance, including the surpassing of your former self.

But if the library is not the nearest thing to the arts, Robert Frost knows well enough what to look for in those who learn at school. He told some senior girls at a finishing school recently that he could tell them what they had learned. Once, he said, parents used to say to their children, home from school, "Well, what did you learn today?" Naturally the children got all self-conscious and could not tell. But he could tell. He could tell them what they had learned in their four years. They had learned to read.

And if they hadn't, if they and their school had failed, he said, they could go to college and be given a second chance. That was what colleges were for, to provide a second chance to learn to read. If you have already learned, you do not need to go. College might be bad for you. You might learn to study what was meant only to be read. And, worse yet, after a long time of that—four years of college—you might leave college to write something meant to be studied. Then you would be contributing to the downfall, decay, and sterility of culture.

In 1945 he talked of how actually we learn to read. In reading a poem, he said, part of the fun is in knowing, already, where everything in it comes from. But that must be made possible by earlier reading— all of it that is not made possible by having lived. It is not fair to the reader to interfere with his pleasure in using what he knows, by the distraction of footnotes.

Poetry is, he said, the purest kind of reading. And what you do, in reading more and more rich and inclusive poetry, is not advancing: it is spreading; it is circulating. You circulate through literature. You spread from a limited range of reference to a wider and wider range. You start, say, with a jingle from Mother Goose. It helps you, later, to read poem number two. Poem number two helps you to read poem number three. Poem number three helps you to read poem number four. And poem number four helps you to read poem number five. Then number five helps you to read number two. You read this time with much fuller identification and delight. And so you go, spreading, keeping up a circulation.

But it must be, must always be, pleasure. "What New Year's resolution did you discover worth taking?" he wrote from Amherst in January 1920. "I resolved not to let anyone put a book to any use it wasn't intended for by its author—if I could help it. Some will ask how they are going to kill three hours a week and not put an occasional book to an occasional use it wasn't intended for by its author. Embarrassedly twiddling thumbs if necessary. Or, if that suggests too much a country courting, let them read aloud a good deal and teach others to read aloud. Shakespeare says good orators, when they are out, spit. There is something that will suggest itself when other things fail.

"Go at it now for genuineness. A minimum of class work and all kinds of work for mere exercise. Remember that some of us have got by without ever having written a thing for exercise. Dorothy Canfield was telling me the other day that she had. She's a Doc of

Phil of Columbia too. Make it real and you'll beat the Dutch.

"I've kicked myself out of Amherst and settled down to revising old poems when I'm not making new ones.

". . . Teaching is all right and I don't mean to speak of it with condescension. I shall have another go at it before the last employee is fired. I believe in teaching but I don't believe in going to school. Every day I feel bound to save my consistency by advising my pupils to leave school. Then if they insist on coming to school it is not my fault: I can teach with a clear conscience."

Though he never read a book through till he was thirteen, Robert Frost is obviously a book-lover. And he desires to see the tribe increase. Once he visited the rooms of students and gave them credit for the number and the quality of the books they bought.

He gets students curious about all sorts of racy, humorous, robust minds, even certain ones called popular. I shall never forget hearing him read Ring Lardner's preface to his "How to Tell Short Stories," or passages from Mr. Dooley. It disturbed my pedantry to observe his pleasure in the story of the devil's wager, heard on the phonograph recording of Bert Williams. And he discusses Damon Runyon and his mastery of a special language. It once seemed different when the "thieves' Latin" or cant was of the time of Villon or Henry Fielding. But Robert Frost was not fooled by such differences. He liked Will Rogers while Rogers was still alive, and called him "the international court fool." And when asked to name ten books he would take to a desert isle, he included, along with the Odyssey and two collections of poetry, Anthony Hope's *Prisoner of Zenda.*

Once he gave a semester course in minor writers. "I don't teach," he wrote that year—1923. "I don't know how. I talk and have the boys talk. This year I'm going to have two courses, one in literature and one in philosophy. That's funny. I don't know that I know much about either. That's the reason perhaps that we get along so well. In the course in literature we're going to read a book a week. They're not going to be major authors, the classics of literature, either. They're going to be minor writers—people that aren't so well known. Why do I do that? For a reason that I think rather good. Those boys will, in the course of their education, get the first rank people whether I include them or not. That's what education very largely means today—knowing the names that sound the loudest. That's what business means, that's what success means. Well, I'd like to get out of that rut for a while. I'd like to get the boys acquainted with some of the fellows who didn't blow their trumpets so loudly but who nevertheless sounded a beautiful note. We're not going to read the works in class: we couldn't do all of that. The boys will do their reading at home. They'll read in class the things that appeal to them most. An incident. A bit of dramatic action. I'll let them choose what they wish; I'll let them read what they wish. And then we'll have some fun in their telling me why they made their choice, why a thing called to them.

"I don't want to analyze authors. I want to enjoy them, to know them. I want the boys in the classes to enjoy their books because of what's in them. . . . Youth, I believe should not analyze its enjoyments. It should live. It doesn't matter what they think Hazlitt thought or tried to do in his works; what matters is the work, the story, the series of incidents. Criticism is the province of age, not of youth. They'll get that soon enough. Let them build up a friendship with the writing world first. One can't compare until one knows."

It was not at all from commentators and systematizers that he asked them to read. He goes always to the original finders and makers: the physicist Bohr for information about the behavior of electrons, Gibbon for his large and daring look and his innocent give-away facts, Mayan explorers, Latin and medieval Latin poets, Darwin in his *Voyage of the Beagle*, Prescott for the conquistadors, Aquinas for a specimen of the way theologians think. The books that he reads through have a man behind them—a man with some kind of flair that shapes his material to form.

At Wesleyan once he talked of the difference between knowing about books and touching literature. "You've got to get down to as much substance as you can. In literature I'd rather know four or five poems than all of anybody's understanding of those poems. (Perhaps that isn't a fair comparison)—than a whole sweep down through six centuries of English literature. I would rather know those few by heart than have anybody use them as stepping stones to give me a sweeping view of those periods. It is the same with Latin, Greek, and history. I would rather touch a few stones that the Greeks left than have a whole two years of explication of those things by somebody.

". . . there is another way to come close to poetry, fortunately [besides writing it; he started writing poetry when he was fifteen] and that is the reading of it, not as linguistics, not as history, not as anything but poetry. It is one of the hard things for a teacher to know how close a man has come in reading poetry. How do I know whether a man has come close to Keats in reading Keats? It is hard for me to know. I have lived with some boys a whole year over some of the poets and I have not felt sure whether they have come near what it was all about. One remark sometimes told me. One remark was their mark for the year: had to be—it was all I got that told me what I wanted to know. And that is enough. I think a man might make twenty fool remarks if he made one good one some time in the year. His mark would depend on that good remark.

"The closeness—everything depends on the closeness with which you come, and you ought to be marked for the closeness, and for nothing else. And that will have to be estimated by chance remarks, not by question and answer. It is only by accident that you know some day how near a person has come."

XVIII

So, he made form

Robert Frost doesn't concede a thing to those who assume a young man writes from a philosophy he learns in college. He says, instead, it is all right for a young man to be interested and excited by what comes under his eye and just make something of that. The piecing together comes gradually, till, when he is older, he has a world.

Philosophy that you accept crumbles beneath you when you are fully exposed to a new situation. It doesn't work then. A truly personal philosophy is a slow growth. And, to be sure, people whose philosophy is formed by slow desiring, seeing, and doing are articulate chiefly in deeds. But a few make known their world in words that are the next thing to deeds. Despite their acquaintance with man's thought through centuries, such philosophers think as formatively as if no previous thinking had been done.

Robert Frost suits actions to the uniqueness as well as the usualness of particular situations. He never got over heeding the difference between the emergent situation and the general type into which it could be classified. The likeness and the difference, together, determine his acts.

This process, though, is seldom self-conscious. In the hours of actually making up the mind, impulse, checked and focused by many emotional memories, projects the action. And the decision becomes a good decision by being made good; made good in the design that, after a series of decisions, can be looked back at and figured out. The design was in the making all the way along, but foreknown "only with some sort of emotion."

It is as if with each commitment "a piercing little star was through." And after a series of decisions

> *On the pasture bars*
> *I leaned to line the figures in*
> *Between the dotted stars.*

Constellations of intention gradually emerge. It is the same for a life as it is for history—or for the meaning of a poet's whole work.

When Robert Frost selected sixteen of his own poems for Whit Burnett's anthology of contemporary writing called *This Is My Best,* he wrote: "I have made this selection much as I made the one for my first book, *A Boy's Will,* and my second book, *North of Boston,* looking backward over the accumulation of years to see how many poems I could find toward some one meaning it might seem absurd to have had in advance, but it would be all right to accept from fate after the fact. The interest, the pastime, was to learn if there had been any divinity shaping my ends and I had been building better than I knew. In other words could anything of larger design, even the roughest, any broken or dotted continuity, or any fragment of a figure be discovered among the apparently random lesser designs of the several poems? I had given up convictions when young from despair of learning how they were had. Nevertheless I might not have been without them. They might be turned out of the heap by assortment. And if not convictions, then perhaps native prejudices and inclinations."

He spoofs himself a little while he states his serious meaning about a poet's meaning. He sits near the tall boys in the back pew; he never speaks from behind an emasculating pulpit. His refusal to claim much is in the interest of openness to yet unrealized incompatibles. It is the opposite of false modesty. I have not known a more complex person, though I have not known one so nearly simple. He likes the world because it is a place where you never know.

XIX

Like a moment of total living

— but lasting

If you see the little truths with sharp delight or pain, you will not be anxiously straining to do final justice to the whole of reality. If you have had it ground into your cells that of all the concerns of dire and of supreme importance no one is lastingly *the one,* you can relax and play with form. When you momentarily achieve it, you will say with Robert Frost, "I enjoy most the state of being in form."

Just for the moment what-seems-to-defy-and-to-deny is incorporated in affirmation; I am free because this arrangement fits for now the transient unity I have in myself achieved.

Form that falsifies no ambiguities is what Robert Frost has always been after. Back in 1916 he said: "While writing the writer should be exclusively interested in the subject matter; when he has finished all he cares about is the form." Returned from reading two Phi Beta Kappa poems at Harvard, he said of "Bonfire" that he liked it for its shapeliness. It is like a Greek vase, he said: it has the flaring lip, the incurving neck, the bulge and the long, narrowing body, and the wider base. It didn't please him much that he had been praised as "protoplasmic"; he privately remarked that using the primary stuff of life was not enough. "Nobody going," he said with a wink, had as much form as he.

In 1929 he emphasized the difference between form and self-expression: "Poetry is measured in more senses than one: it is measured feet but, more important still, it is a measured amount of all we could say an we would. We shall be judged finally by the delicacy of our feeling of where to stop short. The right people know, and we artists should know better than they know. There is no greater fallacy going than that art is expression—an undertaking to tell all, to the last scraping of the brainpan. I needn't qualify as a specialist in botany and astronomy for a license to invoke flowers and stars in my poetry. I needn't have scraped those subjects to the point of exhaustiveness. God forbid that I should have to be an authority on anything, even the psyche, before I can set up as an artist. A little of anything goes a long way in art. I'm never so desperate for material that I have to trench on the confidential, for one thing, nor on the private, for another, nor, in general, on the sacred. A little in the fist to manipulate is all I ask. My object is true form—is, was and always will be—form true to any chance bit of true life. Almost any bit will do. I don't naturally trust any other object."

The form he wants comes without foreordination. Faithful to an initial feeling, he concentrates on the subject matter. Gradually design appears; changes with the conditioning of the technical verse form and the unsparing truthfulness to the subject matter; continues under the modulation of the initial feeling by the commitment to line length, to rime pattern, and to stanza form; and with the achieved correspondence of voice tone, sense, and meter in the last line is for the first time complete. Every sound and shade of meaning is affected by the developing form; every sound and shade of meaning also determines form. The design is *there* only when the poem is done.

A true poem is "A Constant Symbol" of man's achievement of freedom with order, in successive commitments of adventurous and responsible living.

Form requires, as Robert Frost shows in "The Figure a Poem Makes," a feeling that has found its thought to be "wild about." And so the form means more than that which the poet consciously meant to say. It means what he, as a person, means. It discloses him at highest concentration.

Form is almost alive, almost like a time in your life of intense living. And it has one superiority to intense living: it can be grasped and yet act out its own nature and give off new gleams and flashes each time you look at it.

XX

The saint and the artist, unlike the craftsman, wait for the high moment when they are good because grace is added to their best

" 'Style is the man.' Rather say, the style is the way the man takes himself, and to be at all charming or even bearable, the way is almost rigidly prescribed. If it is with outer seriousness, it must be with inner humor. If it is with outer humor, it must be with inner seriousness. Neither one alone without the other will do."

Robert Frost is serious because of caring; he is humorous because intense devotions are funny. The man with style smiles at his own intensity—and so maintains it. Robert Frost in sober earnest was never more serious than when he was joking.

In his talks with would-be writers he kept coming

back to the need for "doubleness." On meeting and providing for ambiguities depended charm, integrity, and worth. For instance, there is ambiguity about the way poets get the stuff of poetry. In his introduction to *The Arts Anthology*, published at Dartmouth College in 1925, he wrote:

"No one given to looking underground in spring can have failed to notice how a bean starts its growth from the seed. Now the manner of a poet's germination is less like that of a bean in the ground than of a waterspout at sea." (Please observe the way he "drives in a peg" to shut off the inadequate metaphor that someone might be expecting him to use.) "He has to begin as a cloud of all the other poets he ever read. That can't be helped. And first the cloud reaches down toward the water from above and then the water reaches up toward the cloud from below and finally cloud and water join together to roll as one pillar between heaven and earth. The base of water he picks up from below is of course all the life he ever lived outside of books."

The reaching down from the cloud, he said, is "about as far as the poet doomed to die young in every one of us usually gets. . . . If he were absolutely certain to do as doomed and die young, he would hardly be worth getting excited over in college or elsewhere. But you can't be too careful about whom you will ignore in this world. Cases have been known of his refusing at the last minute to abdicate the breast in favor of the practical and living on to write lyric like Landor till ninety."

He found several poems and many scattered lines in which cloud and sea joined together and one poem, in the little anthology, in which "the pillar revolves pretty much unbroken."

If water rushed up from the sea to make the true waterspout in his poems, it is not because of any theorem; it is because of insatiable desire. He told people at a Western writers' conference in 1935: "I remember ten or twenty years of writing after I wrote the first poem that I got any personal satisfaction from. Twenty years of it when I was out and in and didn't know what I was and didn't know what I wanted, nor what the feeling was that I wanted to satisfy. Not having anything in the mind, no formula, just seeking, questing."

But he always knew that he must not develop a nose for news, that he must not go after experience of literary value. "A definite purpose, like blinders on a horse, inevitably narrows its possessor's point of view." And, besides, when you know too well what you are out for, you aren't completely *in*. It was no new discovery that made him laugh at the report that Ettor and Giovanitti, radical labor leaders of about 1911, were getting themselves put in jail "in order to keep hard." He had long known that any experience you can remove the sting from by telling yourself how you'll make use of it is phony. Knowing how you can telegraph for funds or resume the gentleman disqualifies. You have to be sunk in the experience. There must be no out except the one you fight for or invent.

He was always trying to confirm the somewhat im-

aginative in their hunch that real experience comes
incidentally:

> *Heaven gives its glimpses only to those*
> *Not in position to look too close.*

"I suppose," he once said, "you ought to write poetry to gratify some feeling that nobody has gratified
for you. . . . The primary thing is gratification . . .
you can't get any other way. . . . You gradually find
what the particular craving, of your own is—that the
other poets haven't satisfied and you slowly eliminate
them until there is nothing left but the pure you. . . .
Poetry won't begin in thought. It may back up in
thought. It begins in a haunting feeling that must be
satisfied. . . . The first thing the mood picks up is not
words . . . it is some urge of an idea to embody itself
in. The idea picks up the words. The words make the
poem. You've got to know the great difficulty of it . . ."
He broke off, amused and sad at the impossibility of
showing anyone who did not already know.

He cares more about the imaginative state, I think,
than he does about more writers. For what goes to
make poetry goes, also, to make meaning anywhere
it's made. It goes for meaning in our lives and in our
country.

One day when he sat in on a class of mine he talked
of the cambium layer in a tree. Between the solid
wood and the protective bark, he said, is what botan-
ists call the cambium layer. If school doesn't put us
through the mill, there's something like it in us. All

around the tree from root to leaf and flower is this thin inner sheath. Through it move the minerals and the sugar. It has its sleep in winter when the frost lasts all day long. The rest of the time it never ceases action, never ceases changing while the tree's alive. It is always solidifying, always expanding. The inner side of the sheath—or ring, as we see its history in the cross section of a sawed-off stump—becomes stiff wood, to lift the tree and hold it erect against the storms; the outer side forms the inner bark. What was the delicate and quick tissue, carrying nourishment and making the new cells, turns steadying and up-raising staff or corky hide, but in between is always the new cambium layer begotten by the old. And the transformation is always gradually going on. Reaching from roots to twigs, it uses what they draw, through root hairs and leaves, from earth and cloud and light. And, by acting on what is taken in, it renews itself and gives off shoots, buds, and flowers.

Sometimes, however, the period of daylong frosts is frighteningly long. That is doubtless why most of the young poets accept their doom and turn practical. Or write by the newest formula.

When Robert Frost was old enough to need lots of sap to keep from being mainly venerable, he told members of the Grolier Club that they could call themselves lucky if they liked. Being craftsmen, they were saved from the "acedia," the apathy and melancholy, of him who waits for something to take shape within. They have an advantage, he told them, over saints and artists; they keep going at their tasks. The moment of access may come to them. It may. But the saint and the artist wait for the high moment when the thing goes without pushing, when they can mount and ride. And in the intervals they seem to be only waiting. And it may not come.

That separates the artist from the craftsman.

XXI

He has, then, the freedom
of his materials

Conflicting emotions of many situations are surprisingly allowed for in Robert Frost. The simple-minded poems are there as having made good on all counts; the simplicity is the real thing that all of us wish for. He has kept himself in such order that he can still be excited when a great many allowances have been made. That freedom has been his chief poetic desire.

Perceptions taken with enough emotion, he knew, would keep. They could be "turned under," they could "build soil." From them, ideas would "occur," as some new hunger or horror shot a twinge or a stitch between them. Even the new idea might be used only "to throw ahead of him," as he once said, "into the future, the way a man might throw stones in front of him in a wet meadow. Then when he wants to strike a course for somewhere across the meadow he can go dry-shod, irregularly straight."

These self-shaped ideas Robert Frost uses in his lectures and in his incomparable conversations. He has been known to use his own metaphor in two different lectures as much as six months apart. For repeated use gives the ideas currency in his own mind and contributes to his freedom among his materials.

As he wrote in an early letter, he changes his grievances about once in six months, and does not esteem them worthy of poetic permanence; so he changes the metaphors he uses in conversation and public conversation about as often, new ones conceived in excitement replacing those well broken in but still fired with his life force. He will use the old ones again, when he needs them. He will be able to "mix them up," as he likes to watch a good baseball pitcher doing. His over-all feeling at intervals becomes so strong that it can revive and correlate all the seemingly incompatible feelings he has had in the past. So when he composes a poem a whole man speaks. It is not mankind speaking. But it is a whole man.

And he entertains so many ideas that repartee is always going on in his mind—repartee, though passionate, committed. That makes possible the answering of voice to voice in his poems, the play of good thought with counterthought. It makes every lyric dramatic.

And so he has the freedom of his materials. And he acceptingly incurs "some dust thrown in my eyes," if that "Will keep my talk from getting otherwise."

All the other great desires—for affection, truth, beauty, power-without-crowding, justice-with-mercy, and continuing chances—are conditioned by his keeping up the swing. I have seen him temporarily and rarely relinquish some freedom to be kind, or to keep an obligation. But he goes through labyrinths for freedom.

XXII

"Enthusiasm taken through the prism of intellect" is his power

You have to dare to be "overwhelmed" to know freedom. Fear you have to live with and be master of: a craving so exigent that no payment in suffering, time, misunderstanding, grief, and loneliness is too exorbitant, is what you need. Gaining the freedom of his materials, Robert Frost disdains unearned privilege and licentiousness, even "poetic" license. In his delicate and moving balance, responsibility is inseparable from response.

But we have to give offense. The best, Robert Frost once said, that we can do—as friend, lover, parent, teacher, or fellow citizen—the best the State itself can do when things go very wrong is to "make it right."

Only one who precariously achieves such freedom is a character. Only one who cares more for order than the merely law-abiding care can take into himself the conflicts that divide his fellows, cause extremes to meet, and so become a shaper and a maker. Only intellect can tame enthusiasm to form.

But intellect can do so only when in it there are no partitions that shut off osmosis, no sticking drawers of stuffed filing cabinets. What often passes for intellect marks "the only materialist . . . the lost soul." For thus Robert Frost characterizes "the man who gets lost in his material without gathering a metaphor to throw it into shape and order."

"I for my part would not be afraid," he said, "to go in for enthusiasm. There is the enthusiasm like a blinding light, or the enthusiasm of the deafening shout, the crude enthusiasm that you get uneducated by poetry, outside of poetry. It is exemplified in what I might call 'sunset raving.' You look westward toward sunset, or if you get up early enough, eastward toward sunrise, and you rave. It's ohs and ahs with you and no more.

"But the enthusiasm I mean is taken through the prism of the intellect and spread on the screen in a color, all the way from hyperbole at one end—or overstatement at one end—to understatement at the other end. It is a long strip of dark lines and many colors." A genuine feeling is mastered without being diluted—"passed through an idea—tamed by metaphor."

Bright impressions are not enough. "Sometimes you are impressed by some bit of what you see," he said while talking to a group of students, "and the impression weaves itself into a poem. But it won't do because it lacks meaning. Other times the meaning is too heavy for the thing. A full and natural union you must have."

Meanings that give value to impressions arise in the lifelong activity of discovering connections. Becoming educated, he said once in a late night conversation, is taking from myriads of experiences indelible impressions and, over the years, discovering, in separate zones and on different planes, impressions joined by filaments of likeness. With him indelibility seemed strongest when he was young. He could hear, he said, in his mind's ear, words, phrases, idioms—inflections and everything—just as they first delighted him. And it is so with many kinds of experience. He has kept himself, and he has continuously become, a whole that he could cut into anywhere. Having made that kind of loose sphere of himself, he has ideas. But the things he writes come, also, from new discovery. Everything very good is a putting together of things connected whose connection has just been seen.

This realization of a new connection is neatly visible in his poem "The Gum-Gatherer." It is a plain case, too, of passing an enthusiasm through the prism of intellect. For thirty years he had been taking indelible impressions about the life of an artist. He had lately had two years of rich association with artists in England. He had reflected much about what bad risks artists were held to be. He had known that relatives and acquaintances had looked on him as no good. But, now, he had begun to demonstrate what he had always quietly believed: that he could make up and more than make up for all his wayward nonconformities. Then one day he encountered a man from the back country among the mountains who made his living by gathering spruce gum. He discovered suddenly that he, the poet, was like a gum gatherer.

THE GUM-GATHERER

There overtook me and drew me in
To his down-hill, early-morning stride,
And set me five miles on my road
Better than if he had had me ride,
A man with a swinging bag for load
And half the bag wound round his hand.
We talked like barking above the din
Of water we walked along beside.
And for my telling him where I'd been
And where I lived in mountain land
To be coming home the way I was,
He told me a little about himself.
He came from higher up in the pass
Where the grist of the new-beginning
*   brooks*
Is blocks split off the mountain mass—
And hopeless grist enough it looks
Ever to grind to soil for grass.
(The way it is will do for moss.)
There he had built his stolen shack.
It had to be a stolen shack
Because of the fears of fire and loss
That trouble the sleep of lumber folk:
Visions of half the world burned black

(as the artist does—
wins you to his rhythm,
and encourages you,
leaving you to act)

(Relation must be
somehow reciprocal
—one reason why
R. F. took lifelong
interest in *where* all
sorts, spiritually,
lived)

(Habitat of artist)

(Artist's raw materials,
too, *look* so)

(Artist *takes* his
freedom. It's neither
provided nor
approved)
(Originality partly
destructive;
iconoclastic that it may
be iconoplastic)

And the sun shrunken yellow in smoke.
We know who when they come to town
Bring berries under the wagon seat,
Or a basket of eggs between their feet;
What this man brought in a cotton sack
Was gum, the gum of the mountain spruce.
He showed me lumps of the scented stuff
Like uncut jewels, dull and rough.
It comes to market golden brown;
But turns to pink between the teeth.

I told him this is a pleasant life
To set your breast to the bark of trees
That all your days are dim beneath,
And reaching up with a little knife,
To loose the resin and take it down
And bring it to market when you please.

(The artist genuin[e]
and ironically
sympathizes with fe[ar]
he will later prove
excessive)

(Without heighteni[ng])

(Completion upon
co-operation of the
enjoyer)

(Like the artist)

(Faithful to real
essence)

(Not on order)

If the reader gets the feelings suggested by the concrete particulars, he will gradually get the feeling of the whole experience, and the universal implications will ooze out in a rough jewel.

XXIII

He excites with sight and insight

One of the evenings in 1945 after a lot of entertaining reminiscences, Robert Frost told about a recent conversation he had had with John Dewey. They had agreed, in different words, about what it took to produce a work of art. He still liked the two words he had so long used: sight and insight. And that night he enriched his old phrase. "First," he said, "you have to be sure, completely sure, what the *thing* is; what is required is sight and insight. Then . . ." He searched the wary faces of the two young writers. "Then, you might add one more, if you were generous about the pun . . . : *ex*cite. Sight, insight—and—excite." You have to get the spark across from the sensation to the significance.

It is the excitement that empowers you to sink your factual missile. It will rankle till the poison spreads.

Robert Frost uses metaphor, the sort you promptly

recognize, more often in conversation than in his poems. But remember he spoke of a man gathering a metaphor to give all his welter of experience form. All his poems come from a sort of central metaphor. Many an individual poem is one analogy, entire. It is sight or sights with the attendant, often unstated, insight. By the tightenings and relaxings, the turnings and the doublings, the departures and returns that are in the verse and, consequently, in the feelings of the reader he implies the insight.

Each poem is a sort of metonymy or synecdoche. The whole poem suggests. In gradually grasping, you pass through "delight to wisdom." In each poem is the climb, in each the swing back down to earth.

And he wants you to get the meaning by touch. He hopes it will be mostly yours when the experience closes. One night after a public lecture at Bread Loaf in 1924 he and Robert Gay and I walked up a sandy road through woods and under stars and talked of how the writer gets going. Back in the years of rejections, he said, he tried drinking as a detonator. For a short time he drank a lot, alone in Boston. It didn't help. A woman poet, he knew, claimed she had to have a man before she could have a poem. She was mixed up, he said, in her conceptions.

What a writer needs, he said as we slowly mounted, is to be able to draw forth the virtue of things by touch, the way the Syrophoenician woman did from Jesus, by putting her fingers on his robe. She got everything—the virtue went out of him—at a touch.

Just touching the hem is enough. Spiritual essences provide the intoxication.

And the subject matter, also, comes by touches. You don't have to have a dozen love affairs to know about love. Never mind if Burns did write himself a note—it's on the margin of a manuscript that Robert saw at Buffalo: "Get some more experience of love before writing any more poems on the subject." He carried out the assignment what you might call *in extenso*. It wasn't necessary. To get the essence of homesickness you need to be alone in a strange land but once. And you don't need to ride a hundred miles an hour twenty times in order to know what it is to "travel." The great thing is not opulence or repetition; it is the sensitive touching of the hem.

Another time he said it was like showing somebody a man in a forked carrot. You don't carve out a face. You do just enough with your thumbnail so that the other fellow sees. Just enough; that's the hard part. "How plain should we be? What proportion of a poem should a child understand? I myself would rather not be misunderstood by so much as a policeman. I am in favor of being understood."

Robert Frost makes sure of the sights—makes his gamble on so placing and arranging them that the reader will have the insights. Yet he does it touch and go. He takes his chance that the reader may not see. For example, you might not know that he is writing on the freedom of materials, that he is saying our hope as mortals is in our power of rearranging, when you read:

I've tried the new moon tilted in the air
Above a hazy tree-and-farmhouse cluster
As you might try a jewel in your hair.
I've tried it fine with little breadth of luster,
Alone, or in one ornament combining
With one first-water star almost as shining.

I put it shining anywhere I please.
By walking slowly on some evening later,
I've pulled it from a crate of crooked trees
And brought it over glossy water, greater,
And dropped it in, and seen the image wallow,
The color run, all sorts of wonder follow.

XXIV

Yet he is homely and parochial

On June 13, 1914 a review of *North of Boston* in the (English) *Nation* said that Robert Frost was "apt to treat the familiar images and acts of ordinary life much as poetry is inclined to treat words—to put them, that is to say, into such positions of relationship that some unexpected virtue comes out of them."

He never dealt with the ideas you have been taught to cross yourself before—as you hasten out of their vicinity. He rarely used—never used without new mischief—the charged symbols in which the play from thing to thought has faded out. No scarab, ichthus, or scepter. He composes with your unschematized experiences—the experiences you had before you were far enough along in school to be awarded filtering goggles. Or he uses experiences that you had thought were in a scheme and takes the scheme apart. He uses the stuff of the experience that burst your plan and would never, after that, quite fit. He uses those memories that have not been stylized in the frescoed tunnel through which education would safely shunt us to the grave.

He uses "the familiar images and acts of ordinary life," because he likes them and finds them full of suggestion and analogy. We have not included them among the topics on which we trust an expert's formula above our own sight and insight. Nor are they among the frail and foreign wonders expected on the private grounds of poets.

I say he uses "your" experiences and memories. It is his pride to hold fast the impulses, sensibilities, and passions that initially belong to the ordinary man. They belong to him until he adapts his sensibilities, and passions, to fit some least common denominator of unobjectionableness. A thing that, we should note, is done as much and as injuriously by us who graduated with high honors and keep always safely and honorably within approved limits as by the man who stops school at the fourth grade.

Robert Frost has made himself at home. His pains and pleasures gradually have made themselves at home in him. He makes himself at home with his world (though no world is easily accommodated to the very sensitive, and some who might contest his sensitiveness pride themselves on always living not at home). He seeks to make other people at home with him, and makes himself, as far as they will permit, politely at home with them.

His is homely poetry. And if we democrats in the

United States still have a greater reverence for the heavenly or the courtly, a forelock-pulling subservience before the cosmic or the global, so much the more need of him. So much the more convenient, also, paradoxically, for his insidious effect. With our slight depreciation of what is domestic and familiar, we shall be less on guard; possibly poetry may stretch its out-of-fashion boots before our kitchen fire.

After the fact, Robert Frost saw how his native preference complied with his desire to see poetry once more a power. If poetry could reveal the difference between loveliness and glamour and prove the price of that difference well worth paying, then it could do without the bated breath and the bared head. Let it suffer the ignominy of being unsuspectingly taken for granted: just local, from around here somewhere, nothing cosmopolitan or Frenchified or high-toned in any way. Poetry makes good as it becomes part of common sense. It is a way to make the finest, highest, and most gleaming keep coming back to alight on the road from home to work.

In 1926 he told the boys in my writing class that the aesthetic range was from exquisite beauty, through elegant beauty, homely beauty, rough beauty, terrible beauty, mean beauty, to vile beauty. He had never been able to go to vile beauty, he said. He knew his limits. Shrubbery in spring with a lot of manure and straw around the roots was beautiful to him. He could go that far. That was a well-dressed garden. But in general he swung a little this way, a little the other way—as the balance of things required a shift —somewhere near the center of the scale.

"Attempts to heighten or dignify the facts do not succeed." It is no palliation of the drudgery of daily repeated household tasks "to call a broom the wand of Hertha, the hearth goddess. One who behaves himself must not be afraid of the ordinary; he must call a broom a broom." He said so on a night when we stood looking across at moonlit white clouds against the horn of Mount Lafayette. He was, as he once praised a lesser poet for being, "just rough enough with beauty to show a man's assurance that beauty can't get along without him."

Besides, he couldn't bear to leave out the broad to prevent the subtle from being missed. The subtle didn't come separate from the broad. Nor would he, if man could, see so far that he could no longer notice the lesser ambiguities. He would not be a blind and blundering foreseer; he would not inhabit any "isle of the blest" suspended over the garden of his neighbor.

Nor would he have the delicate differences of feeling diluted by estimable but secondary feelings. He disliked words already redolent as a lady's dresser drawer. He has never allowed a literary nimbus to obscure actual mist fronds. He won't let the pleasant musk of an old book smother the smell of clover in down hay.

It's true that old themes newly ordered can be as sumptuous as vestments shown to tourists in old churches; they can be as refined as a carved ivory back-scratcher. But Robert Frost is "apt to like a poet who writes about unusual things—it seems to me the best proof of a real poet. Moons and running brooks have been written about over and over again. Anyone can borrow them out of a book. Then again it is easy to write about certain traits of character—generosity and heroism for instance. . . . However there are shades of character which are harder to see and when a man notices them. . ."

When a man notices them he writes not angrily realistic poetry; not even systematically realistic poetry. It may be the kind of sensing the real that self-avowed realists never do. It may be "The Black Cottage," caught "in a sort of special picture" and "fresh painted by the shower a velvet black," so that for the first time in your life a long-unpainted house with "rank grass" through which "The path was a vague parting" is " 'Pretty,' " and the little old lady who long since lived in it is neither lavender and old lace nor New England decay, but one of the unpredictable and complex people whom transients seldom get to know.

Robert Frost let the critics label him "poet of New England." He likes knowing the world through layers of growth and weather, of quirk and character in one section. But he lived his most impressionable years in San Francisco. He spends much of his life in university and college towns, including two long stretches at Ann Arbor. He says he knows the city better than the country. Those years in unideal but very industrial and very American Lawrence surely count. So does a considerable stay in London.

He touches the center of people's natures by his power of knowing some of them a long time in New England, and he gets intimations of ideas "we haven't tried" while watching men and growing things and watching, also, ice and snow. But he rightly confesses himself "the author/Of several books against the world in general." And he is what he is at least half because of being, as he wrote in a London poem, "Acquainted with the Night."

XXV

His aim is "in singing not to sing"

Part of his luck is in having what he calls "a good forgetter." He doesn't carry his own failures long. "You have to live by shedding," he says. "You would never move your spirit to a single dance step if you didn't have a good forgetter. You get rid of things by acts and phrases. Milton shed his frustration about his blindness by the phrase, 'They also serve who only stand and wait'; he could go on and write *Paradise Lost*."

Reading his poetry would help us forget. Not that he gives us lullabies. But he would divert us from our private failures by making us enter into other people's feelings, which he evokes by the sounds of their speech.

Between our first and second dishes of ice cream, in a drugstore in Littleton one day in 1922, Robert remarked that there should always be people in poems. Yes, even in lyrics. Lyrics ought to be dramatic. A poem ought to be something going on; not mere description or ejaculation—action.

There is always at least a protagonist in a poem of his. He always takes us beyond the printed page to people or a person talking. Reading with what he calls "audile imagination," we hear their tones and inflections. We get to know the person as he is at the given moment and, back of that, infer his whole personality. If there are two or more people, we see (or rather hear) how they affect each other. And we perceive, along with the more tangible facts of the situation, the subtle drama that is taking place between them.

The lawyer in "The Self-Seeker" is, for instance, so calloused by his training that he sees only the legal facts and misses the tone and all that it half reveals. We, the readers, have the fun of watching the emotional inappropriateness of what he does or says. We feel the affection of the friend opposing the literal meaning of his words. And we share each character's different experience of the single event. At last the conflicting sympathies are pulled together, though we're still haunted by the little girl who so carefully preserved the orchids, by the maimed lover of flowers who can never again seek the rare ones far and wide, and by the friend who can't bear to see him signing for such paltry damages. Perhaps those tones will finally have given us a more poignant sense of the inadequacy of all solutions. Perhaps they will strengthen a bent toward sympathy.

Good dramatists and story writers, verse or prose, have usually had an ear for speech meaning. Robert

Frost goes further. He says the only live sentence is one with the living voice somehow caught in the syllables.

I suppose it serves him right that many highly educated people don't know how to read his poems. They are terrified of anything a fool might mistake for exhibitionism. Their own talk is as flat and noncommittal as they can make it. And they uncritically assume that scientific findings have displaced and discredited emotional realizations. Anything unstatistical is too vague and relative to be trusted. And so some ears are paralyzed for poetry—especially the poetry of Robert Frost. Many apparently don't hear the way people talk. When they try to read aloud they monotonize. And the identification with another person that accompanies fitting our throats and tongues to his emotions can't take place.

Robert Frost early detected this tendency and opposed it. He enjoys reproducing the tones and inflections he heard people use before he was ten years old. He has, ever since, satisfied his curiosity about people by listening to their give-away speech. He has remembered shades of difference.

"I first heard the voice from a printed page," he once said, "in a Virgilian eclogue and from Hamlet." From that time his writing has consisted of "images to the ear." In 1935 he was saying: "Poetry has to do something to you with sound. I do not care about meaning except as I use it to get meaning out of tones of voice. . . . The tones of voice can only be got by the context."

"They call me a New England dialect poet," he said late in his career. "Not so you'd notice it. It was never my aim to keep to any special speech, unliterary, vernacular or slang. I lay down no law to myself there. What I have been after from the first, consciously and unconsciously, is tones of voice. I've wanted to write down certain brute throat noises so that no one could miss them in my sentences. I have been guilty of speaking sentences as a mere notation for indicating them. I have counted on doubling the meaning of my sentences with them. They have been my observation and my subject matter.

"I know what I want to do most. I don't do it often enough. In 'The Runaway' I added the moral at the end just for the pleasure of the aggrieved tone of voice."

But earlier, in letters from England and Franconia in 1914 and 1915, Robert sent me his thoughts about voice sounds and sentence sounds. Reading extracts from those letters along with his poems of those days and today will indicate why poetry is an art distinct from music, though akin, and why he chose "in singing not to sing."

"The living part of a poem is the intonation entangled somehow in the syntax idiom and meaning of a sentence. It is only there for those who have heard it previously in conversation. . . . It is the most volatile and at the same time important part of poetry. It goes and the language becomes dead language, the poetry dead poetry. With it go the accents, the stresses, the delays that are not the property of vowels and syllables but that are shifted at will with the sense. Vowels have length there is no denying. But the accent of sense supersedes all other accent, over-rides it and sweeps it away. I will find you the word 'come' variously used in various passages, a whole, half, third, fourth, fifth and sixth note. It is as long as the sense makes it. When men no longer know the intonations on which we string our words they will fall back on what I may call the absolute length of our syllables, which is the length we would give them in passages that meant nothing. . . . I say you can't read a single good sentence with the salt in it unless you have previously heard it spoken. Neither can you with the help of all the characters and diacritical marks pronounce a single word unless you have previously heard it actually pronounced. Words exist in the mouth not books." (January 14, 1914.)

"It may take some time to make people see—they are so accustomed to look at the sentence as a grammatical cluster of words. The question is where to begin the assault on their prejudice. For my part I have about decided to begin by demonstrating by examples that the sentence as a sound in itself apart from the word sounds is no mere figure of speech. I shall show the sentence sound saying all the sentence conveys with little or no help from the meaning of the words. I shall show the sentence sound opposing the sense of the words, as in irony. And so till I establish the distinction between the grammatical sentence and the vital sentence. The grammatical sentence is merely accessory to the other and chiefly valuable as furnishing a clue to the other. You recognize the sentence sound in this: You, you . . . ! It is so strong that if you hear it as I do you have to pronounce the two yous differently. Just so many sentence sounds belong to man as just so many vocal runs belong to one kind of bird. We come into the world with them and create none of them. What we feel as creation is only selection and grouping. We summon them from Heaven knows where under excitement with the audile imagination. And unless we are in an imaginative mood it is no use trying to make them, they will not rise. We can only write the dreary kind of grammatical prose known as professorial.

"A word more. We value the seeing eye already. Time we said something about the hearing ear—the ear that calls up vivid sentence forms.

"We write of things we see and we write in accents we hear. Thus we gather both our material and our technique with the imagination from life; and our technique becomes as much material as material itself.

. . . .

"You aren't influenced by that Beauty is Truth claptrap. In poetry and under emotion every word is 'moved' a little or much—moved from its old place, heightened, made, made new. . . . I want the unmade words to work with, not the familiar made ones that everybody exclaims Poetry! at. Of course the great fight of any poet is against the people who want him to write in a special language that has gradually separated from the spoken language by this 'making' process. His pleasure must always be to make his own words as he goes and never to depend for effect on words already made, even if they be his own." (December 1914.)

(Such words as flatter, forlorn, immemorial, alien, incarnadine, Robert Frost would never use as they are used in the great lines in which they were first made.)

"Remember, a certain fixed number of sentences (sentence sounds) belong to the human throat just as a certain fixed number of vocal runs belong to the throat of a given kind of bird. These are fixed, I say. Imagination cannot create them. It can only call them up for those who write with their ear on the speaking voice." (February 2, 1915.)

XXVI

Keeping tangent always

to common sense

Poets who desire, like Robert Frost's Eve, to add to the common voice "an oversound," their "tone of meaning," have gladly taken part in the world of feeling and common sense around them. But at the same time they have to do much of their living tangent.

He had been telling, late one night at South Shaftsbury, one of the apocryphal tales—about Jesus and Judas and the schoolmaster. A writer, he said, in a new biography of Jesus tried to make out that Jesus had a sense of humor. No, he said, Jesus was a man of sorrows, not a good fellow or a humorist. Humor is the beginning of doubt. It's defensive: you're not going to let them get you, let them know where you are sensitive. But the very religious nature is not humorous, not on guard. That is just what bothers you in people who lack humor; they are not on guard enough. They're always exposing themselves.

I had been reading a novel by one of the earnest. I admired it. It looks at many levels of life, I told him, and makes its main character move toward a satisfactory understanding and aim, by a series of disgusts and a series of identifications of himself with physical and psychical degeneration.

Robert's nose wriggled. He shook his head, smiling.

"Wasserman has got down to the place for a new beginning."

I stuck to my borrowed oversimplification. "He enters into the feeling of the fellow who ravished and caused the death of the hero's generous and joyous friend—a girl whom the hero loved without desire."

Oh, that German thing, Robert said. He had looked into it. A stinking slime of speculative magnanimity. It triumphs over all human abhorrences. A decent man would have destroyed that filthy, spoiled creature—consumed the nasty mess of rottenness in a blaze of anger. One of the things he had always cried for in his heart, he said, was the unavenged injustices. We cannot shirk the responsibility for judging and condemning. There was a great advantage in the old way of avenging crime, some injury done your kin or neighbor: immediate reprisal.

He saw my frown.

Avenging was done in the heat, he said, and seemed fitting. Cold-blooded official justice is less fit. But— it's less likely to make mistakes. Shutting them up for life may be the best way. But such festering creatures must be separated. You can't save gangrene.

He mussed his hair. Executions are bad for the

executioner. That's the worst of executions. Think of making a living at a hundred dollars a kill. They used to let them remain unknown—brought them in from obscurity for the occasion.

But novels like that he hurled from him. No sense speculating on how to get perfection. If Wasserman wanted to postulate, it would be more interesting to have his main character say: Since God let all this evil be in the world, why not take all of it into himself, unless God would stop him? He might see what would come of that—for an idea.

Robert slid still farther forward and down in his chair. It's too late, he said.

I looked at my watch. Ten minutes of two.

It's too late, he repeated, in the history of the world, to start all over new—to expect to find some theory that will get everything in.

Robert Frost has always been keeping his toe in the door so important truth would not be shut out. And yet he contradictorily insists, repeatedly, that we cannot harmonize all of reality, ever. No hope of finding a way to keep all the rotten apples in the barrel. He swings. He's for more inclusiveness than philosophers achieve; he's for eliminating what we plainly can't incorporate, in practice. This inconsistency—this refusal to pretend to be logical and complete—is the fierce, radical trait that makes Robert Frost.

There is no such thing, he said, as making a reconcilement between all the perversities and diabolisms and what is relatively sound. It has always been too late.

They'd better give up perfection, he said. The main good sense of life is an accumulation of generations, roughly vindicated by time: a gradual rounding out. It is globular; not square, but a loose solid. Common sense, we call it.

A writer goes to pieces, he said, if he loses contact with that globe. A very few, like H. G. Wells, can kick themselves off away from it a few thousand miles, to take a look at it from far. It takes some tremendous inner explosion. But they come drifting back, pretty soon. In fragments and flakes. Not whole themselves, nor with a whole idea for a new mankind.

But all artists go a little way off—and come back. Tangential. The globe of common sense shades off into vagueness on its periphery. That margin is the interesting part for all the arts. A poet is mainly occupied there. But the majority of mankind sleep at the core. Thought masses are the same as matter masses. It's during the eclipse that you see the corona. You need the ordinary globe of sense. No globe, no corona. The great figures of speech are struck tangent.

XXVII

Putting a straightedge on a curve

Robert Frost does not believe statements, by introducing chairmen, about his influence on the spirit of America. He feels a constant share in the shrewd and generous Yankee common sense. He also enjoys the treasure of poetry that he has by heart. Putting his own curve on a traditional technique, rich in American passion and reaching back to archaic Greece, he delights to give a new contour to the old cornucopia. For him, real poetry has to have a doubleness besides the kinds we have been thinking about. It must have the tones of natural speech *and* be metrical. You get it fully when you respond to "meaning struck across the rigidity of meter."

Mechanisms always threaten to choke off the breath of man. But no one can avoid necessity. We cannot do without machines and organizations. And so anything entertaining or artistic that doesn't come to terms with the necessary is frivolous. It begs life's main question: How can we participate in a world we did not design, and still not sell out?

Robert Frost once told me, as we drove along the curves of the Wild Ammonoosuc, that he liked anything that puts a straightedge on a curve. Such form is true to the conflict of law and liberty. He thought he could conform and yet take liberties. A real feat, he called it, to prove that in spite of law and order a man can do "what a man will put into effect at any cost of time, money, life or lives."

He can make rime and meter serve to carry out his intention more exactly. His conforming is transformed into a "flourish." It takes high spirits to juggle on a tightrope, exuberance in conditions that might sterilize and stiffen. A poet is a man of such high spirits that, after all the other conformities— "conformity to the dictionary, to grammar and to the conventions of thought and of life"—he still has "excess energy." He has "more than enough" to conform once more, still "without compromise."

To claim exemption from limitations, to demand unfettered expression, is to insist on staying at bat after one has swung three times. So measure must be given to vagueness that there may be meaning. Man provides measure in his collaboration with the wind that bloweth where it listeth. The almost inaudible underbeat of the metrical accent affords a south-wind serenity even in the face of a north-wind fact. Meter and rime relate what is frightening, because new, to the old reassuring regularity. The friendly familiarity of measured sound steadies us in the moment of new perception. No matter where the now limited wind may move us to, we are still within the area of that familiar beat.

In lyrics, rime enhances the security. The casual talk of characters provides it in Robert Frost's blank verse. In reading the blank verse you miss the poetry unless your ear controls your accent and inflection. You're at a loss without eager memories of the way folks speak. And in reading the rimed lyrics, you may hear too much of the return of similar sounds, and think some mechanical, if your ear doesn't tell you how to say it.

Your audile imagination tells which rimes are brought out by a strong accent on the riming syllable, and which rimes should be scarcely heard. The meaning insists that most rimes stay faint. Only those come full throat in which something culminates or consummates.

"The great art is to make them so that they couldn't possibly be missed," Robert Frost says. He does not always succeed. But his whole life and all his poetry accept a responsibility that other human beings are free to frustrate. There would be no prowess if human beings were readily responsive.

Robert Frost talked publicly one time about his "claim for poetry." He claims that it is "beyond the ideal." The ideal, he says, is what we can't stop wanting. The Sermon on the Mount cannot be put into practice. Christians all recognize its impracticability. But we can't let it alone. We can't stop wanting what it bestows blessing upon and what it proposes. It is ideal. Good! No belittling of ideals. But poetry goes beyond the ideal.

A poem is a fact, *factum*, a thing done or made. It reconciles things of which most of us are content to say: "In an ideal world they would go together. It would be nice if things were that way." In a good poem they do. "The fact is the sweetest dream that labor knows." *Fiat*, the poet said, and it is. That is the way with a good poem. It is, for all, not for the writer only, fact, act, deed, fulfillment, proof.

XXVIII

It is a matter of corresponding

There was a time in his youth, Robert told me once, when he was like the dog breeder who told Borrow that he was shipping twenty fighting dogs to the Pope o' Rome. Popes and everyone would be dog breeders if they could, he said. Robert once supposed everyone would be an artist if he could. But a businessman he met on a boat opened his eyes. The businessman took it for granted that all men would be in business if they could. So Robert got over thinking that we were all balked artists. But he never lost his mischievous impulse to start all sorts of people putting things together like a poet.

> *I could say 'Elves' to him,*
> *But it's not elves exactly, and I'd rather*
> *He said it for himself.*

For poetry to set people thinking as an artist thinks, it must be a pleasure. In 1946 he mocked at "reading with a grub hoe." He was gravely confident of the gift of one of his friends who seemed to be turning to such poetry. "His were the real thing. He was one of our best," he said with a sad smile. But withdrawing into obscurity was no good. He shouldn't be disheartened because the larger public failed to understand. Being difficult was all right; willing obscurity was all wrong.

A poem that had "a barb to it and a toxin that we owned to at once" could be granted unlimited time to produce its full effect. "The utmost of ambition is to lodge a few poems where they will be hard to get rid of, to lodge a few irreducible bits. . . ."

One such irreducible bit that is more than communication is his "Blueberries." I find in it no explicit ideas, except the playful exaggeration,

'Who cares what they say? It's a nice way to live,
Just taking what Nature is willing to give . . . '

But the poem puts me in correspondence with the husband and wife talking together, reveling in the memory of picking berries together, remembering how they accused each other of scaring away a bird from its nest, how the woman feared after long silence that her husband "had wandered a mile" and shouted and he answered "as low as talking" when he "stood up beside" her, and how they enjoyed a fellow feeling with Loren and his berry-picking family who knew no berrying place (" 'I'm sure—I'm sure' "—as polite as could be'). The love of growth and of living as I have known it comes over me with a reassurance and an impetus never found in books— like this one I am writing.

For a writer to have this power he must be good at corresponding with the nature of things. He must feel in himself the thirst of plants and the probing of roots. Or he must catch himself stiffening when some-one is being reprimanded, or chuckling and feeling relaxed when the father catches on to what a boy says out of the corner of his mouth. He knows how animals and people feel—perhaps even has intimations of storm and weather changes, by going through the same thing inwardly as he watches.

In a million ways he may correspond sympathet-ically, both with the inorganic strains and stresses and with the organic growth, struggle, and decay. And he must have been on both sides, also, of innumerable human conflicts.

He gets his material from correspondences between himself and the nature of things, including other peo-ple. He becomes a container of more and more con-flicts, and he composes them.

In the same casual way he finds out how his poten-tial audience can come to share his endurings, over-comings, and composings. By matching himself over and over to the acts, gestures, tones of many and varied people, he comes to know in his pulses and his impulses how to move them.

Then comes the poet's third kind of corresponding.

Having known the nature of things by fitting his sensations and exertions to nature's processes, and having sympathized with many varieties of other people by unconsciously matching their motives and reactions, the poet sets—more consciously—about causing readers to desire and to do the kind of corresponding with him that he has, all his life, been doing with the external world and with people he has cared about. By sounds composed in skillful ways he induces readers to match him. They "take" things with him for a moment. They discover with him "what to make of" things.

But it's advantageous to be "versed in country things." Country realizations ingrain the ambiguity of life, set up opposite feelings, each as valid as the other.

Robert Frost would neither be "afraid of nature" nor "besotted with it." He saves his power of strong emotion by cauterizing sentimentality. He knows cruelties that are full of joyous possibility, and joyous possibility that is destroyed if the cruelty is not left possible. Once all the feelings are composed, the problems of the hour shrink into actual situations to be acted in—without gestures longer than your arm.

Robert Frost has always cared about the feelings that produce another's tone. By dramatic suggestions he can put his readers into similar correspondence with a character. We get inside the angry hay hand in "The Code" and cannot stand off in horror at his deed. Old feelings of ours are called up and combined as we read:

They realized from the way I swabbed my neck
More than was needed something must be up.

In "The Fear" we know just how she felt when we read:

She spoke as if she couldn't turn.

Such correspondences operate more through gestures, tones, silences, frowns, stiffenings, flushes, flinches, and glances than through words. And to make words catch their meaning is to be profounder than philosophy. When farmers read Robert Frost's poems with correspondence, it is because he has seen and felt the poetry in their lives. "The farmer on his Sunday holiday," he said in 1921, "is apt to stray out just to scratch the back of his pig or to salt the cattle. It is a little ceremony—a kind of poetic ceremony—tender like. You know after a severe winter a farmer will go out to his trees and proceed to pick off a few blackened buds, and there is a little poetry in that, more or less—a practical thing to be sure—but another little ceremony into which enter the elements of poetry."

It was on that day that he remarked: "We have had nature poetry for a hundred years. Now we must have the human foreground with it."

Of course, he is content with congeniality less than perfect. People reveal themselves in response to his gentle sympathetic seeking, just as all human knowledge has come "In answer to the mental thrust":

Eyes seeking the response of eyes
Bring out the stars, bring out the flowers.

We all seek something akin to us, something with which we can find correspondence. The poet seeks it everywhere he goes, and he writes effectively by making use of our desire to correspond. We all begin that way.

"We begin in infancy," Robert Frost wrote in 1935, "by establishing correspondence of eyes with eyes. We recognized that they were the same feature and we could do the same things with them. We went on to the visible motion of the lips—smile answered smile; then, cautiously, by trial and error, to compare the invisible muscles of the mouth and throat. We were still together. So far, so good. From here on the wonder grows. It has been said that recognition in art is all. Better say correspondence is all. Mind must convince mind that it can uncurl and wave the same filaments of subtlety, soul convince soul that it can give off the same shimmers of eternity. At no point would anyone but a brute fool want to break off this correspondence. It is all there is to satisfaction; and it is salutary to live in fear of its being broken off."

XXIX

And that requires separateness

that is tough

Correspondence, he said, "is all there is to satisfaction." But he also said: "Keep off each other and keep each other off." We feel the twinge of ambiguity. We are mature beyond the taste for dry wine when we can agree to both.

"A poem must have in it some relation to the topics of the time, it must have something in common with the editorial pages of the United States at the time," he said. "This means significance." Yet when eager boys asked him in 1944 what he thought about the race problem, he told them he preferred to disregard it. And most of them—too cheaply rescued from their confusions by altruistic formula—never realized what he meant. When he was with an Eskimo he met him as a person, not as a digit in a problem. But the illiberal liberal boys never notice that people cannot be corresponded with as union member, editor, one of the rich, Mississippian, or proletarian. Touch is between persons. And the best thing you can ever do for others is be a person yourself and treat each of them as one. Problems are fictional oversimplifications; people can be social, if each of them is a person.

Minds meet by risking the very differences that are suppressed in coming to a compromise. In real meeting the differences "strike" and enhance the interest. If you have known and loved a person for what he is, you know that nothing possible in this world—no exemption from anguished pity, no guarantee of peace and comfort, no insurance of the pleasures of eating, sport, and sex—nothing can compensate for depersonalization of persons. For all those things, especially sex, gain all their human value when person corresponds with person. We

> *must bring to the meeting the maturest,*
> *The longest-saved-up, raciest, localest*
> *We have strength of reserve in us to bring.*

Such reserve takes toughness. The totalitarian leader shows a sort of toughness when he calmly lets the girl he loves be executed. She has not obeyed the latest directive from the central committee. But he is not so tough as that.

Early in the 1930's I stood on the terrace Robert Frost had laid in front of his second house at South Shaftsbury one darkening evening. Robert looked very grim. The plug-uglies would be having their way, he said. The fine people were not tough enough.

The fine people, he said, give up their other desires in exchange for security. They get large new concepts or select new dogmas. They attach themselves to the modern mind, and so have less and less mind. They are so busy with what is being said, thought, and written that they have neither energy nor time to make discoveries. They are among "the first to be second."

The fine who are not tough eviscerate themselves, he said, in spewings of unrelated sensation, in novel after novel. They pule out faint shames and fears and oh-dear-me's in occult verse. Their manner is some-one else's—in France or England. Perhaps they go and tell a psychiatrist their dreams and run back their sewage to their reservoir. Perhaps they fellow-travel. They are all really nice people. Only they didn't avert the imposing of a ready-made world when they were young. They were not tough enough.

XXX

But tough separateness
is none the less social

Robert Frost never accepts as the social metaphor either cowering or stampeding. "We are chasing something rather than being chased," he told one of his large audiences at Harvard in 1936. "Now and then we shy away from something, left or right. Guide right, guide left—like a snail with its feelers." He held up two twiddling fingers until people in the audience seemed to sense the quivering, exploring feelers.

"We," people; "we," Americans; "we," mortals on this earth. Robert Frost's "we" is elastic. Whether you are included or not depends on you. He thinks you are, unless you decline to be. He is discovering for us all. He is "an ordinary man."

The "we" doesn't come apart because you go to the left when something on the right puts you off from your desire. Only, you mustn't cease to use your feelers. There will soon be something to guide away from on that side. And the thing you and we are all chasing is not there. Shying is continuing the pursuit. Turning squarely and marching left or right is treating what you shy from as pursuer. Doing so, you give up. For the only way not to be a victim is to keep pursuing.

And, each time, after shying from something, left or right, and resuming the forward course, you will belong to a smaller "we." But, unlike fugitives, who continue to the right or to the left, you will not count as enemies those who are not included in the smaller "we." Only the indefatigable pursuers belong continuously and without forgetting to the biggest "we" of all, the "we" of people, right and left, and crippled along the map.

Not that pursuers of meaning are altruists. They have ample egos. One evening in 1916 some reminiscence of his politician uncle in Lawrence started Robert talking of selfishness and society. The social order is based, he said, on sacrifices on the various planes of selfishness. We give up on one plane to gain on a higher. But in such sacrifices we are still trying to satisfy a desire that is selfish—of the self. For the family we make sacrifices on all but that highest plane of the spirit on which no sacrifice could be made. For the state we sacrifice on a low plane of more material things. And in all social intercourse we renounce a selfish desire on one plane to gain on what seems to us to be a higher one. A generous person is not less of an ego than a petty person. He embraces more.

But if you are contributing to the social good as a self-seeker, getting selfish satisfaction from being social and belonging to the big "we" of the United States and of all the world, you need the fortitude to bear loneliness. Robert Frost had the thought in his poem "Bereft" near the start of his lifelong chase, when he was eighteen years old,

> *Word I was in my life alone,*
> *Word I had no one left but God.*

He never forgot.

It sets him free from cadging, goose-stepping, or domineering—free to be truly considerate, co-operative, and social. Knowing how alone we really are, we shy from certain separations and shy, again, when they at last take place; we never become fugitives from loneliness. We keep renewing our pursuit.

And we won't get so systematic in our chase that we can't keep changing direction with our quarry. We will be after form, and we don't let plans prevent continuing pursuit.

> *May something go always unharvested!*
> *May much stay out of our stated plan,*
> *Apples or something forgotten and left,*
> *So smelling their sweetness would be no theft.*

We never reach what we are after. "The utmost reward of daring" is "still to dare." The form we achieve is for the sake of better form. And the accidental beauties that we happen on are precious, for us and for all whom we can persuade not to trust laying out the future. There's

No place to get lost like too far in the distance.

Those who are running after and not from can pause to show a way through down timber to those next behind. And they find the moments and the places in which the brief loveliness appears.

It's guide right, guide left for the one who is not pursued. Now it's "Provide, Provide"; then it's "Let's have a look at another five."

But the real thing is never the sure thing—not quite sure. He had to be either a victim or an adventurer. A challenge masks in spoofing, in

It seems immoral to have to bet on such high things as lives of art, business or the church. But in effect we have no alternative. None but an all-wise and an all-powerful government could take the responsibility of keeping us out of the gamble or of insuring us against loss once we were in.

XXXI

Though not like a reformer

Robert Frost is sure that poetry should, like teaching, be a matter of touch and go—of lodging something way beneath the skin and vanishing. He has himself always known that, the more stuff and stamina a person has, the less he will be told.

In 1948 he remarked to girls at Bryn Mawr that poetry offers "tentatives but no tenets." Tenets you hold with rigor. Tentatives you try; when new knowledge demands, you change them. Poetry offers tentatives and declines to supply safeguards.

The tentatives come from inborn tunes sung but once and not quite through to the end, and heard when we are not on guard, "almost before the prick of hostile ears." For instance, Robert Frost writes of a prize pullet in terms of "the fancy." He gives vent to his lifelong enthusiasm for top-notch living things, with power, charm, self-reliance, fertility, and style.

And his pleasure in the winner of "A Blue Ribbon at Amesbury" just runs over enough to suggest a trifle more.

> *The night is setting in to blow.*

> . . . . . .

> *The lowly pen is yet a hold*
> *Against the dark and wind and cold*
> *To give a prospect to a plan*
> *And warrant prudence in a man.*

Soon after Robert Frost became a celebrity he was engaged to read—the first poet who had ever been hired—at a dinner of the Poetry Society in New York. A lady who sat near him conscientiously explained that she was not a regular attendant.

"Staying away won't hurt you," he said.

"That sounds cynical," she said.

"No, spiritual," he said. "The spiritual life is lived when we are by ourselves."

"I had thought of it as doing good," she said.

"The spiritual is different from the social though close to it."

And if you come to spiritual perceptions, you may see that security cannot be externally set up. In "The Old Barn at the Bottom of the Fogs" the security was all external, a pair of chestnut props the only way of fastening the doors. The spaces between the boards were only pencil-wide. And the tramp who slept there far from houses woke to find it

Like waking in a cage of silver bars.

He didn't like the threat of propping security from the outside.

. . . it had almost given him troubled dreams
To think that though he could not lock himself in,
The cheapest tramp that came along that way
Could mischievously lock him in to stay.

Security should mainly be determined from within. But one of the strongest human propensities is minding other people's business, Robert Frost says. And the only hope of thwarting it is in minding our own.

XXXII

His friendship gains by being selective

Not entangling himself with organizations, Robert Frost could be neighborly. He could happen on his friends in likely and unlikely places. Being sure himself that it is a poor and sentimental gamble "to try if one more popular election" will bring the next thing to the millennium, he has stayed a friend to some who hoped temporarily to put politics before poetry, external order before internal form, existence before life.

For his part he has always been too cynical to be lured into materialism by a heavenly light. He was never fooled by the claim that if you made people healthy and comfortable they would grow sensitive, discriminating, and noble. He has never believed that first things stay first if you put them second.

He knew by experience that outdoor plumbing didn't interfere with being an artist. When his income was high he had no more of the best in life than when his income was low.

But he has been the lifelong friend of some of the less decisive whom he teased. "To be social is to be forgiving," he wrote. He doesn't go around voicing his forgiveness, but he forgives everywhere he goes. One way he said it, in 1948, was, "Damn them, damn them all . . . but we must forget that." With people as with things that he loves, he loves them for what they are.

He gives a casual few human beings what idealists postpone to Utopia: the pleasure of being liked for what they are. It is just a happening. And there are reticences. He keeps his best friends sufficiently strange, he says, so that he can entertain them. And he likes people whom he finds entertaining. He told my writing class, one April day when he made them forget the rain for two hours, that the person he liked most on his latest visit to California was a humorous rascal who seemed to like only the greatly bad. "He's on the wicked side, of course," he said; "but he's witty and alive."

Merit has very little to do with it, he said another time. He has hardly ever become friends with any-one if something interfered with a good impression at the first meeting. It wasn't a list of qualities he liked; it was composition—a different composition in each instance, with different flaws and flairs. Usually there was some flair—even if it was no more than a "kind of spirituality."

One friend I heard him tell about admiringly was

a not very scrupulous but intelligent and kindly Irish-American lawyer. He had a large and liberal mind. Once Robert said to him that they could say anything to each other without compunctious awe of authority or creed. His friend stiffened. He stood in righteous awe of the displeasure of the Church, the lawyer said; and he would rejoice in his heart if he were granted grace to be instrumental in Robert's salvation.

Robert has always reserved the right to be openly amused at his friends' absurdities, and the more tried the relationship the more unsparing is his teasing. Part way through his public career someone questioned whether he had many friends. The accusation reached his ear. "So much the better for the few, I think," he wrote. "Don't you?" He keeps most of his early friends and gains new. No matter how long the intervals between meetings, the give-and-take picks up when they do meet, as if the separation had been only overnight.

And his friends have always been more numerous than was generally known. They belong to various strata. One, for instance, is a railway mail clerk who used to give Robert a lot of stories about farmers in Vermont. He knew everybody and all their affairs. He knew who owned what pieces of land and when the title changed. He viewed his fellow mortals in the valley of his run with a detachment that was "creepy," Robert said.

Whether his friend is poet, college president, member of "the undeserving poor," federal judge, newspaper man, ambassador, or farmer, Robert regards him with detached attachment. One of his closest friends was Edward Thomas, the English essayist and critic, whom he persuaded to write poems. Robert did not hesitate to say that the poems were not so good as they were praised for being—when Edward Thomas was dead—by fellow poets who treated him scurvily while he was alive. "Romancing" about Thomas annoyed Robert. But his detached recognition of the real man made all the stronger the attachment reticently shown in "To E. T." and in "Iris by Night":

One misty evening, one another's guide,
We two were groping down a Malvern side
The last wet fields and dripping hedges home.

.   .   .   .   .   .

And then there was a moon . . .
Then a small rainbow like a trellis gate,
A very small moon-made prismatic bow,
Stood closely over us through which to go.
And then we were vouchsafed the miracle
That never yet to other two befell
And I alone of us have lived to tell.
A wonder! Bow and rainbow as it bent,
Instead of moving with us as we went,
(To keep the pots of gold from being found)
It lifted from its dewy pediment
Its two mote-swimming many-colored ends,
And gathered them together in a ring.
And we stood in it softly circled round

From all division time or foe can bring
In a relation of elected friends.

For those who dare to know ambiguities, "it seems as if" holds truth unavailable in any laboratory.

XXXIII

And love by accepting ambiguities

One day in 1911 as he and I walked down toward one mountain interval, Robert remarked that Shakespeare could teach more about love than all the lecturers; even the bawdy passages would help us more. Love was to Robert passionate and private. He would not exhibit or cerebrate. Sex can be overt; love is covert. He thought that in correcting nineteenth-century anemia we impoverished love.

"It is by a sort of metaphysical gradient. There is a kind of thinking—to speak metaphorically—there is a kind of thinking you might say was endemic to the brothel. It is always there. And every now and then in some mysterious way it becomes epidemic in the world. And how does it do so? By using all the good words that virtue has invented to maintain virtue. It uses honesty first—frankness, sincerity—those words; picks them up, uses them. 'In the name of honesty let us see what we are.' You know. And then it picks up the word joy. 'Let us in the name of joy, which is the enemy of our ancestors, the Puritans . . . Let us in the name of joy which is the enemy of the kill-joy Puritan . . . ' You see. 'Let us,' and so on. And then, 'In the name of health . . .' Health is another good word. And that is the metaphor Freudianism trades on, mental health. And the first thing we know it has us all in up to the topknot. I suppose we may blame the artists a good deal, because they are great people to spread by metaphor."

When he was seventy an acquaintance tried to twit him. "What you need," the man said, "is an aphrodisiac."

"You're disturbed," Robert replied, "because I won't write *you* one."

But he never was one who knew "the line where man leaves off and nature starts too well for any earthly use." "Fastidiosity" he always mocked at. Neither was he, for that, deprived of realizations known only to the fastidious. To be sure, man and woman had something in common with buck and doe. Woman and man could feel warmly akin to the doe and the "antlered buck of lusty nostril," in "Two Look at Two." And when they were alone,

Still they stood,
A great wave from it going over them,
As if the earth in one unlooked-for favor
Had made them certain earth returned their love.

But people can have more than the best they share with the wild and shy. They can have less. They can have less because they are wild but not shy. "The Discovery of the Madeiras; a Rhyme of Hakluyt" is one of Robert Frost's fiercest poems. The

> captive pair
> *Whose love was such they didn't care*
> *Who took in them onlooker's share*

as reported in the tale of the Captain of the former slaver, were little more than "a savage jungle cat" and a tom. It was cruelly fitting that when the male came down with fever and "the girl fought them and made a scene," the thought should come

> into someone's head
> *Of the ocean bed for a marriage bed.*
> *Some Tom said to Dick or Harry:*
> *'Apparently these two ought to marry.*
> *We get plenty funerals at sea.*
> *How for a change would a wedding be?—*
> *Or a combination of the two,*
> *How would a funeral-wedding do?*
> *It's gone so far she's probably caught*
> *Whatever it is the nigger's got.'*
> *They bound them naked so they faced*
> *With a length of cordage about the waist,*
> *Many lovers have been divorced*
> *By having what is free enforced.*
> *But presence of love these had in death*

To kiss and drink each other's breath
Before they were hurled from the slaver's deck.
They added clasps about the neck
And went embraced to the cold and dark
To be their own marriage feast for the shark.

At least they had their wildness to the last. Their
passion was real. The other woman in the poem had
the desirable shyness, but lacked the wildness. She
was not wild enough to be sure of her feelings and
pay all the price. Her death was worse. She came near
having the human overtones that the Negro lovers
missed; but her humanness wanned into the apathy
sometimes mistaken for spirituality.

When her lover forcibly lifted her into the pirate
ship

The way she clung to him the more
Seemed to argue perhaps she went
Not entirely without consent.

It was never more with her than "seemed," "perhaps,"
and "not entirely without." She was on a pirate vessel,
but she was "a lady." And when her husband "in a
moment of cross unruth" yielded to her faint but persistent questioning and repeated the Captain's story
about the wild lovers,

She withdrew back in self-retreat.

She faded and kept on fading after her lover had got

the Captain to let them off on "a nameless isle." The ship first waited and then "sailed and left them."

> . . . *slowly even her sense of him*
> *And love itself were growing dim.*
> *He no more drew the smile he sought.*
> *The story is she died of thought.*

Without the wildness, the human extra did not flourish. The wildness without the shyness was merely wild. Both pairs failed of the lucky composition sometimes (imperfectly) achieved, and repeatedly achieved. But the stolen lady and her lover were at times "like any two."

> . . . *she and her lover would sit opposed*
> *And darkly drink each other's eyes*
> *With faint head shakings, no more wise.*
> *The most he asked her eyes to grant*
> *Was that in what she does not want*
> *A woman wants to be overruled.*
> *Or was the instinct in him fooled?*
> *He knew not, neither of them knew.*
> *They could only say like any two,*
> *'You tell me and I'll tell you.'*

Robert Frost was never taken with the doctrine that people should make any and every compromise to mate. There need be nothing terrible about lifelong continence, he once declared. People profoundly versed in country things knew stunting could be harmless. What was not harmless was getting up, and acting by, formulas.

In "The Subverted Flower" a nice boy and a fine but educationally frightened girl are standing out where goldenrod and brake are waist-high, but within calling distance of her mother's walled garden. He has just made a loving gesture toward her, impelled by a wildness akin, he feels, to the lovely wildness of the flower in his hand.

> *She drew back; he was calm:*
> *'It is this that had the power.'*
> *And he lashed his open palm*
> *With the tender-headed flower.*

The actual flower becomes his emblem of the wild attraction. Without anyone to tell him, he knows that if they do not fear the wildness that is in them both, they will still share the wonder.

> *He smiled for her to smile,*
> *But she was either blind*
> *Or willfully unkind.*
> *He eyed her for a while*
> *For a woman and a puzzle.*
> *He flicked and flung the flower,*
> *And another sort of smile . . .*

a cynical one, came over his face and he sank to creature. But her loveliness lifted him and he held out his arms.

> *'If this has come to us*
> *And not to me alone—'*

But his passion brought her cynical miseducation into focus. She heard her mother call. She waited in stupefied fear. He became animal to her and, because to her, to himself.

> *A girl could only see*
> *That a flower had marred a man,*
> *But what she could not see*
> *Was that . . .*
> *. . . what the flower began*
> *Her own too meager heart*
> *Had terribly completed.*

So the boy stumbled off. He tripped, caught himself with his hand, and laughed sardonically, sounding like a dog.

Then the denied wildness in her tore loose. When her mother got there she

> *wiped the foam*
> *From her chin, picked up her comb*

and, against her will now,

> *drew her backward home.*

Less visibly, the like has happened to many a couple, in and out of marriage, because one lacked the gambling wildness to believe in the flower and not subvert it.

"Love," Robert Frost said to me when neither of us was either old or young, "Love is an irresistible desire to be irresistibly desired."

XXXIV

Even in marriage we enjoy oppositions

Secondary motives march us up the marriage aisle. But flouting social approval indicates a flaw in sympathy. In one of Robert Frost's poems a man of fine impulses, generous nature, and enthusiasm for the prize poultry that he loses money on has been living for fifteen years with a young woman who came as his "Housekeeper." Her wise and competent chair-ridden mother lives with them. As she understandingly explains what has happened, it appears that John is an idealist irreconcilable to the way things are on earth. And, now, Estelle has run off and married another man. Whenever her mother said

> *' "Why shouldn't they be married,"*
> *He'd say, "Why should they?" no more words*
> *than that.'*

He seemed to feel that marrying would put a worldly stain on something better than the world.

But it wasn't "something better" for Estelle. She turned from him because he angrily disdained approval and she couldn't keep on without it.

The crude common-sense world was nearer right than the idealist—as so often. His composition failed to balance. Taste, kindness, and a grain finer than the world demands are not enough. He lacked the imaginative play. Marriage is a decent recognition of one's neighbors. It doesn't guarantee much—love least of all. And "Marriage is not sacred," Robert Frost said, "if a bad marriage can't be broken from." It is a holding from within that makes it sacred.

Sometimes, as in "The Hill Wife," loneliness and unshared fears, especially when "work" is "little in the house" and there's "no child," prepare for "The Impulse," and the man learns of "finalities besides the grave."

The husband might have had more feelers out. It's beside the point to call her flighty. It would have been vain to argue. We can't exclude peril with a ring. We can keep the peril just at bay. But the lucky who keep regaining their balance, steadying themselves for the duel toward unity, never settle down—not all the way down. When imagination is in the love it finds how

> *Not to sink under being man and wife,*
> *But get some color and music out of life.*

But even in a playful marriage there are times

when one is (or both are) like the narrator in "The Thatch,"

> *Out alone in the winter rain,*
> *Intent on giving and taking pain.*

Clashes are of course intensified by caring. Indifferent independence is not possible, no matter how forcibly asserted. And it is not an unhealthy sign if for a while it seems that both are too proud and stubborn ever to give in. Even in a quarrel there can be play. And by a humor-fostered fluke they get around the obstacle.

A sensitive and affectionate husband, like Joe in "In the Home Stretch," has moments of qualm when the two of them have taken a big step together—like moving to the country from the city, or giving up the security of a position to concentrate on writing poems. Did she come for him?

They have to gamble that common purposes rise from shared desires. Robert Frost remarked one night, walking up a dusty road, that if he asked someone to go for a walk and the other assented, he was going to assume the other came because he wanted to. But he had to gamble. He could be mistaken.

There are times that go to make up the ambiguous adventure of marriage when one refuses to yield and the other likes the refuser all the better for it. Women are not pretending when they try to keep their men from danger; sometimes, though, they like them better when they won't be kept. In "Snow" Meserve's wife wouldn't say good night over the telephone when he called her up halfway home through the blizzard to say he was coming on the rest of the way in spite of a hospitable offer of shelter. He was very gentle in his persistence. And his way of calling her showed the affection and good understanding between them.

Mrs. Cole tried to persuade him to stay and tried to elicit co-operative persuasion from her husband. She was plainly thrilled by the thought of the risk and the daring. (The storm was just short of being "a man-killer.") But she tried hard to despise Meserve and to hold that it would be preposterous for him to go.

If you read the poem, you will see how anxiety, and later joy at Meserve's safe arrival at home, unite the Coles, yet how to the last they fence, he playing what he divines about her feelings against the equally genu-ine but contradictory feeling that she utters. The ambiguous whole of their mutual attitudes composes to a skillful and affectionate relationship. Such love never settles. Yet it is full of trust.

Meserve wasn't the only one who had to take chances. Cole took chances, too. A woman is more unpredictable and softly ferocious than a storm of snow. Her challenge is subtler. And Meserve, also, had a wife to face. But he could not stay, though a rationalist would not understand what made him go.

The power of love more than doubles our triumphs over waste. It gives "The Master Speed."

> *No speed of wind or water rushing by*
> *But you have speed far greater . . . .*

Two such as you with such a master speed
Cannot be parted nor be swept away
From one another once you are agreed
That life is only life forevermore
Together wing to wing and oar to oar.

And for earth that is better than unity.

XXXV

And his country, too, he
quizzically cherishes

Robert professed sometimes not to be committed. He was "just a spectator." The only things he had ever committed himself to, he said, were God, the home, and the State. And just as he is competitive in baseball and tennis, he is competitive as an American. He sympathizes with those natural and common motives—so easily risen above in cocktail conversations and on better-world committees—that have, so far, won for nations passing prominence. He never went along with the cerebral Wilson in his claim of being too proud to fight. It has never seemed incredible to him that men in business should want to win markets from competitors in other lands. He looks with indrawn chin and comically appraising eye at any who profess to have no desires at all except the well-being of others.

Americans might as well be good sports, though. I

remember how it chafed him the way we Americans "blackened the enemy" in the First World War. The devil is on both sides, all sides. We might learn to be better sports.

But no one could ever start an American movement with ideas like his. It doesn't look tremendous enough, and in practice it is too everlasting and too difficult: to use all-you-are to accomplish what you really want; to keep going full and mutual relations with those nearest and dearest; to be a kindly and competitive-co-operative neighbor; never to elbow, never to crowd; to be an enthusiastic though skeptical citizen of your native country; and to do your hundred-and-fifty-millionth part to help your country be as decent and considerate as possible with nations who are and should be different.

What Robert Frost knows about himself requires him to grant a little indulgence to his neighbor; what he knows about New England (or California) requires him to be a little indulgent of people in other states; and what he knows about stupidity and cruelty and the seeking of unfair advantage in the United States requires him to be a little indulgent of the rest of the world. A little leeway he grants; a little he expects.

Despite all the disgusts and horrors agitating those outcriers who mistake the nature of existence and the immaturity of us human beings for special curses of this country, America deserves affection. It deserves the affection of the little boy—"His cheek smeared with apple-sand"—who made the poet his friend in

"Not of School Age." And it deserves the affection of the most mature.

Like all things earthly, it is limited; but it is lucky. "The best continental cut in the whole world, all the land between two oceans in the zone most suitable for active men," Robert Frost reminds those he talks with. And, emphasizing as usual the then neglected part of truth, he says the Second World War showed, if nothing else did, that the very things that Alexander Hamilton was blamed for wanting had helped to make this country the most powerful in the world. Waste of natural resources and deterioration of our population by unrestricted immigration had been charged against us. But it was our great freehanded industries and our abundant, vigorous population that had enabled us to do what we had done toward victory.

He never shared the sentiments of his aunt "who used to talk long and loud about the foreigners who were taking over this country." One early memory that deepened his affection for America was of hearing his mother tell of her reception in this country, when she came, "An immigrant,—from Edinburgh in an old vessel that docked at Philadelphia. But she felt the spirit of America and became part of it before she even set her foot off the boat. . . . She was sitting on the deck waiting for orders to come ashore. Near her some workmen were loading some Delaware peaches onto the ship." Peaches are prohibitively expensive and rare in Scotland. "One picked out a peach and dropped it in her lap. 'Here, take that,' he said. The way he said it and the spirit in which he gave it left an indelible impression on her mind. 'It was a bonny peach,' she used to say, 'and I didn't eat it. I kept it to show my friends.' Looking back would I say that she was less American than my father? No. America meant something alive and real and virile to her. He took it for granted. He was a Fourth of July American, by which I mean that he rarely failed to celebrate in the way considered appropriate. She, however, was a year-around American."

So he laughed at his aunt, proud of ancestors who came to America in the 1600's. She stood at her window every Sunday, "behind the curtain," watching "the steady stream of men and women pouring into" the immigrants' Catholic church. "Her mouth would twist in the way that seems peculiar to dried-up New Englanders and she would say, 'My soul!' Just that. 'My soul!' All the disapproval and indignation and disgust were concentrated in those two words."

And Robert Frost sympathized with the "Granny" from colonial days when young Stark called her up in "The Generations of Men."

'... There ain't no names quite like the old ones though,
Nor never will be to my way of thinking.
One mustn't bear too hard on the newcomers,
But there's a dite too many of them for comfort.
I should feel easier if I could see
More of the salt wherewith they're to be salted...'

America would provide the salt, he knew. "New England," he said, "is constantly going through periods of change. In my own state, in Vermont, I mean, there have been three distinct changes of population. First came the Irish, then the French, and now the Poles. There are those among us who raise their hands in horror at this. But what does it matter? All these people are becoming, have become Americans. If the soil is sacred, then I would say that they are more godly in their attitude toward it. The Pole today in New England gets much more out of his plot of ground than does his Yankee neighbor. He knows how to cultivate it so that each inch produces, so that each grain is alive. Today the Pole may not be aware of the beauty of the old Colonial house he buys and may in some cases desecrate it, but three generations from now, two generations, his children will be proud of it and may even boast of Yankee heritage. It has been done before; it will be done in the future.

"And if there are poets among these children, theirs will be the poetry of America. They will be part of the soil of America as their cousins may be part of the city life of America. I am patient with this jealousy of the old for the young. It is change, this constant flow of new blood which will make America eternally young, which will make her poets sing the songs of a young country, virile songs, strong songs, individual songs. The old cannot keep them back."

Robert Frost long since decided that man will not be elevated by one who sets himself that task. So he counters Emerson's assertion that

> *The God who made New Hampshire*
> *Taunted the lofty land with little men.*

He says,

> *If I must choose which I would elevate—*
> *The people or the already lofty mountains,*
> *I'd elevate the already lofty mountains.*

But his love is no astigmatism. New Englanders are funny to him. He doesn't hesitate to call some of them "dried up," or to tell of silly pride.

"I was amused years ago by the form this jealousy of tradition will take," he said. "One of the most brilliant pupils in the class at college was the son of a Polish farmer. Everybody admitted his mental superiority. But the old New Englanders would not swallow the pill as given. They sugar-coated it, by backstairs gossip, which insisted that the real father of the boy must have been a Yankee."

But America has for its whole history been a place to come to in pursuit of that which daring men and women are always after. And that makes America the more lovable.

IMMIGRANTS

> *No ship of all that under sail or steam*
> *Have gathered people to us more and more*
> *But Pilgrim-manned the* Mayflower *in a dream*
> *Has been her anxious convoy in to shore.*

He'd like to see our idiosyncrasies held fast. If only all parts of the United States would hang on to their differences! "The worst of it is," he long ago wrote to me in Montana, "that the difference between East and West or between this country and Europe seems to want to be blotted out in colleges. . . . I say let's try to get hold of what we have here however accidental and then hold on to it to the exclusion of everything foreign the importer has a pocket reason in importing."

If Americans wanted to hold on to their democratic venture in politics, they could. He knew he would ask nothing better. Politics, he said in 1950, like much besides, is cyclical. A lot of people seem to hope that instead it is a progress. The condition that they assume will last is a disappearance of all government in a state of communism, where everyone gets a full dinner pail and full enjoyment and full opportunity for growing grand. That, they tell themselves, will come after government has helped everyone until it is no longer necessary. But a closer look reveals that the next stage to our democracy is one-man rule once more. You have to admit that history contains the series: one-man rule, rule of a few men, limited monarchy with privileges wider spread, republic with a still larger few keeping control, and democracy. Then one-man rule again.

There is plenty wrong with the working of democracy. But it is the best in the cycle. And if we wanted to, enough of us, we could arrest the cycle there. It requires a clear and incorrigible purpose to arrest a cycle. It will swing on. But Robert Frost would do what he could to arrest it about where it is—holding a little tighter here, a little more relaxed there. It is a good bet, he said with a quick solicitation, for those who care enough.

But he couldn't alone commit his country. No more could he, an artist, set it down. He loved too many bits of America to suppose it a graspable unit. Neither he nor any man can state it. He pretends to discover on a pair of his shoes the taste of Atlantic salt on one and Pacific salt on the other. Their "Record Stride" has soaked in representative tastes and spanned America, if anybody wants to fool himself with generalization.

Meanwhile he reminds us in a poem at once patriotic and true that it was repeated deeds of war that won the gift of our country, as it becomes itself, and becomes ours.

XXXVI

It's too bad, but bearable, that nations waste so much in war

Existence is spending and saving—of breath, energy, time. Spending and saving. That is existence, not living. Living is different. Living is forming something that does not waste. It is forming what you "would not part with" and can claim at last that you "have kept," as Robert Frost says in "I Could Give All to Time." A man has to spend profusely to give shape to what he saves. So, likewise, does mankind. And lavish spending looks like waste. It is not waste when it results in a shape of character and worth. But the generous spending needful for producing a shape of meaning has to be so unschematized that there is actual waste.

The United States is beginning to have significance enough so that we no longer feel inferior, colonial, and crude. The accumulation of outright gifts by the long succession of sons that have died in our wars is giving us character. People and land are at last becoming integral; we belong to the country, now, as it has long belonged to us. By deeds of war the potential United States, for which her sons of six or seven generations provided the deed of gift, is becoming. This Robert Frost wrote, in 1935, in one of our country's true poems of history and prophecy.

Even the waste of war can provide glorious stories that are true. It can enhance. Horrible it is. But it can be tragic rather than futile. Worse than war is apathy. "It would be too bad," Robert Frost said to some naval trainees in 1945, "not to care about anything enough to fight for it." But he refused to get up any unit purpose that all the soldiers of the Allies could subscribe to. He just thought them

> *blessed with the acumen*
> *To suspect the human trait*
> *Was not the basest human*
> *That made them militate.*

He prophesied no glorious consequence. He smiled at the talk of an end to wars.

"The longest peace in China will end in strife," he wrote long before trouble broke out there. But he also smiled at the conceivable change in human ways that might—you never know—mean no more world wars. That change might not be improvement. Enforced fictitious unity would be worse than war. Even when nations subordinate their wildness enough so that only a minority of the lawless use guns for taking things and when those few can be taken care of by police and courts, the wildness will still have to have an outlet. There will be conflict as long as there are such incompatibles as gravity and aspiration. If more and more people can take into themselves more and more conflicts and play them . . . we might see what that would produce. Meanwhile we don't want to avoid bloodshed by becoming bloodless. We have to pay for being vertical, as he says in "The Flood."

But if "power of blood itself releases blood," if being what we are as human beings entails waste and suffering and anguish, why should Robert Frost write gloating poems about the fact? Because he is entertained by the lifelong enterprise of finding "what to make of a diminished thing." And, liking that, he does not want to see people deceive themselves about what life affords. He chuckled good-naturedly as he told, in 1945, of hearing a woman on Key West say what later he put into the mouth of Jesse Bel in *A Masque of Mercy:* "Isn't it the saddest thing in the world that bravery is the greatest thing in the world?" He likes a world where bravery is called for. He likes the fibrous and supple character that our ambiguous world sometimes evokes.

We have to take it a little at a time, he'd say, not "too much world at once." And it would help if we got tastes before we had to take torrents. It is with such a thought that the father in "The Bonfire" calls his children:

'*Oh, let's go up the hill and scare ourselves,*

As reckless as the best of them tonight,
By setting fire to all the brush we piled
With pitchy hands to wait for rain or snow.
Oh, let's not wait for rain to make it safe.

. . . .

And scare ourselves. Let wild fire loose we
    will. . . .'
'And scare you too?' the children said together.

Then the father tells them about his fright and his
furious struggle when a grass fire got away from him,
once, and "spread like black death on the ground,"
and how he

    'couldn't bide the smother
And heat so close in; but the thought of all
The woods and town on fire by me, and all
The town turned out to fight for me—that
    held me.'

And he put it out.

    'Why wouldn't I be scared remembering that?'
    'If it scares you, what will it do to us?'
    'Scare you. But if you shrink from being scared,
    What would you say to war if it should come?'

. . . .

    'Oh, but war's not for children—it's for men.'

. . . .

    'Haven't you heard what we have lived to learn?
    Nothing so new—something we had forgotten:

War is for everyone, for children too.
I wasn't going to tell you and I mustn't.
The best way is to come up hill with me
And have our fire and laugh and be afraid.'

It was his own four children and his wife who made him ineligible for the first American draft that came soon after that poem. But he seemed glad to see a graduate student volunteering a few months after his poem was in a book. And again in 1942 he declined to share dejection about young Americans.

"I can't go along," he said, "with people who think this country is in such danger. The boys won't have an easy time at first—they can't have. For the boys from the colleges it is bound to be hard because a whole generation of them have been taught in course after course that a man was a fool to fight in war. They've heard that over and over and it's hard at first—bound to be. But it's something that's got to be done—no doubt about that—and they're learning that, too. I remember some officer of our troops a long way back saying that in the morning we fought like boys, at noon we fought like men, and in the afternoon we fought like devils. And don't let them tell you these college boys are soft—I've seen too many football games. They're not soft."

But he knew about those who are in some ways soft, too. In the First World War one of his very best friends went to war and balked his father's repeated efforts to put him in a safe spot behind the lines, just because he had to convince himself that he was not soft. Shortly before he enlisted, irritated friends had been calling him pro-German. He died in combat at Vimy Ridge. Later Robert Frost wrote in a poem "To E. T." of his regret at missing the chance

> *Through some delay, [to] call you to your face*
> *First soldier, and then poet, and then both . . .*

Long before he knew bereavement from war, Robert Frost knew, as he showed in "Range-Finding," the tension and the terror and how, regardless, life goes on, affectionate and predatory, beautiful and sinister —as it was before.

There's no easing the tragic possibility. But facing tragedy we achieve a meaning. And the possibility of being all but impossibly brave cannot be spared from life, even if man should become too mature for total wars.

XXXVII

We're after ultimates, but we have to content ourselves with individual composings in the main

But Robert Frost has carefully embarrassed all attempts to treat him as an authority. He doesn't, he says, feel very confident of himself. He isn't, as he once angrily affirmed, "any Jesus Christ." He has always known he "might be wrong" in what he thought. He doesn't have the answers—though that has never kept him from making his response.

Where another man's need conflicts with your love, he says need must be first. But he is a proof, in his own life, of the practicability of reconciling work and play, love and need. I probably have as many serious and confidential talks with men as anyone, and sooner or later each of my confidential acquaintances has come to the issue: if one could really do what one really wants to. That is every man's great issue. It is the issue upon which, even more than upon gifts, greatness depends. Robert Frost has for the forty-one years I have known him made love and need all but one. He has withdrawn where he could not do what he wanted to do. But not from life—just from easy and spurious success. His work has been "play for mortal stakes."

He has always been "after ultimates." Why weren't we all? If we were, we had to be cagey. We couldn't afford to shoot ourselves toward what we took for one ultimate in any rocket. Usually, when we commence to leave the earth—really intense and *exalté*—then is just the time to keep our poise, fling out, and kick our way down through the air to the ground.

It made him sadly ironical in 1948 to see men he admired and was fond of turning "from dreamer to schemer." Poets who became program makers and schematic planners were damaged. It was as terrible to be a schematic schemer as it was to be a scheming schemer. The former, also, insidiously involved the latter. The strong were content with composition.

Like all of us, Robert Frost doesn't miss by much being ridiculous or pathetic, a fool or a failure. He has had "varying opinions of" himself. There has been evidence of his unwitting failure in more than half of what might well be man's second obligation. And no intelligent human being could approve of or assent to his every act or thought. Far from it. If he has been wiser and capable of more enduring performance than most of us, it is because he has been too skeptical to trust explanations, too impudent to sink to desperate conclusions, too unintellectual to rest on knowledge, too mischievous to cease adding to the "story," and too lazy to quit gambling that "What set us on fire and what set us revolving" will continue.

Freedom of his materials for him includes the operation of all the feelings, sights, insights that he has ever had. We all talk of facing facts. Not so many of us are concerned about how many facts we keep in view at once. When all the parts of Robert Frost— past, present, and concern for future—were not in play he was not free. All in play, he has been prevented from going the full length of any pity or recoil; earlier pities, earlier admirations, enthusiasms, joys, have checked the gesture. Meanwhile they intensified the experience. He is insufficiently objective to see only what at the instant is glaringly apparent. His objectivity has to reconcile the immediate object with all that is in his world.

He knows too much of the good that comes from evil and of the evil that worsens with efforts to destroy it. He knows too well what happens to the man or woman who adopts "solutions" for "chief problems." It is often a greater disfigurement and a sadder waste than a thousand people suffer from low wages and poor nutrition. He knows too well the injury to whole populations of exclusive accent on physical comfort and material well-being. He has had too many spiritual realizations to be taken in by any schemes for arranging man's affairs so that there will be no more poverty; he couldn't welcome the grand impoverishment of worth. He has never worked out the sum: How many eased existences does it take to equal a life worth living?

But at his lowest and angriest, when he was "ready to say . . . that pretty nearly everything is vanity," he has never quite forgotten "a short list of things that aren't." His part in the play is helping people find out "what to do/With their ever breaking newness." His part is reinforcing, by illustrating, "their courage to be new."

For Robert Frost has not contracted the current low-grade infection. He does not find the highest tolerable delight in a foot-gone-to-sleep tingle such as satisfies the disillusioned, who, the other day, expected to perfect the world en masse. He does not vaguely fondle the hope, either, that general low spirits may betoken a religious pregnancy. Tingling numbness and stunned confusion don't portend a grand enlightenment. He would treat them as we treat a foot gone to sleep. And we had better mind each his own business, not awaiting a glorious universal reception into Abraham's bosom, or anticipating such resolution of oppositions that males and females shall be alike and day indistinguishable from night.

It's a book of misery, Robert said as he gave me back—late one night in May, in his room at the Inn —the little volume of foot-gone-to-sleep verse that the stamp of approval had been smeared over. I wonder why they like misery, he said. It never seems much of an emotion to me. Botheration and misery, those two never seem to have any artistic value. A man ought to free himself for emotions that have more force. It's not sorrow, just misery.

As we talked I was dimly remembering the galvanic

lecture I had just been listening to. It seemed so much more momentous and profound than Robert's reading of a few poems, with light asides, in the same auditorium three hours earlier. Seemed but was not, if you sensed the implications, if you saw how clearly Robert was teaching the essentials of poetry in those few words—which the freshmen boys enjoyed without alarm. Not if you felt the depth of serenity and the large composure that he had more than ever at seventy-odd; not if you yielded to the little simple-seeming poems that he read with gusto and the precisely right degree of reticence and feeling.

"Dr. Niebuhr said tonight that there is a serenity beyond tragedy that is possible but not easy," I said, quoting what was to me a platitude, to see what he would say.

Tragedy, yes, Robert said. There is always tragedy. That is what life is. But you must have heard me say a good many times that nothing is so composing to the spirit as composition. We make a little order where we are, and the big sweep of history on which we can have no effect doesn't overwhelm us. We do it with colors, or we do it with a garden, or we do it with the furnishings of a room, or we do it with sounds and words. We make a little form and we gain composure.

One of the ways that goes far back into history, Robert said, is designing coins. Some of them are crude, of course, and have no form. But from the earliest times most of them have it, have design. They're always, or nearly always, circular. And within that little circle you make an animal or a face or some human figures, with proportion and appropriateness. . . . They are very lasting. We say verse lives "So long as man can breathe, or eyes can see"; but it probably ain't so. Coins last longer.

Some men, he went on, try their composing where it's harder—with people and events. They are often baffled, and they are thrown back on giving order to stones or colors or something more controllable. Then they play the rhythm of meaning against the meter in the verse. And out of the stress of one against the other comes the higher meaning. The meaning that is beyond ideas. That is not too metaphysical. Is it? He put his two hands together and moved one closed palm inside and against the other. . . .

There's no such thing as progress. His nose wriggled up. There isn't a single human quality in all the ring of traits—power, love, craft, faith, rivalry, loyalty, ingenuity, courage (he held the ring between his upheld and facing palms), all of them—there isn't one that could be much increased without throwing the rest all out of balance. It's an iron ring. Try to improve things by accenting one of them: its opposite will be accented somewhere else. Soon we have the proportions re-established. So much love, so much rivalry, so much ingenuity, so much inertia. An iron ring.

But there are flowering times—Greece, Rome, Byzantium, Spain, France, England, and so on. Then the iron ring glows. It seems to become golden, jeweled, many-colored. But it's not progress. Rome wasn't so good as Greece, by general consent. . . . And before that, too, of course, Babylon, Assyria, Phoenicia, Egypt. Egypt two or three times. Flowering.

One of the people, a hero king with a lot of lesser, subordinate manipulators, was daring enough and ruthless enough and charming enough and skilled enough in the common interest to do his composing with masses of people and forces of human passion and manipulated events. Pericles was one such. Just for a little time, of course. Then the ring of human traits was iron again, not gold; an iron ring. But for a little golden time—the Periclean Age—a great flowering with philosophers and artists, and a general color and glow. . . . Washington was one of ours. He made his form with people and large social forces. That was our flowering time if we have had it. It would be nice to think we had one coming.

But all the time, inside all that rush, that sweep that we can't control, are our loves. Apart from the sweep are our art and our love affairs and our teaching and our friendships—all the loves that make meaning in our lives.

It was a warm and friendly evening. I did not say much. But I was happy. After a while I looked at my watch. It was twelve.

Robert said he would go with me. He needed more exercise. He reached for his high old-fashioned shoes. And soon we were walking around the campus green. The lamps were aureoled with mist.

I like this, he said. It's English. We went down Main Street and round the block to College Street. In front of the Inn we got into my car and I drove home.

Had we any beer? Robert wanted to know. I was sure we hadn't. But I looked. He came in. I offered him a grapefruit. He took the squeezer and squeezed it into a cup. I was about to do it without anything to catch the juice, he said. He washed his hands at the sink, his hat still on. Then we went out. I walked with him back to the corner.

It's a lovely night, he said, a lovely spring night. Wet and lovely.

We talked of our next time together—perhaps in July—shook hands, and said good-by.

He wasn't much bent; still sturdy, he walked slowly up the hill. He would be swinging more birches.